Software Quality Engineering

Software Quality Engineering
A Practitioner's Approach

Witold Suryn
École de Technologie Supérieure
Montréal, Canada

IEEE PRESS

WILEY

Published by John Wiley & Sons, Inc., Hoboken, New Jersey.
Published simultaneously in Canada.

For general information on our other products and services or for technical support, please contact our Customer Care Department within the United States at (800) 762-2974, outside the United States at (317) 572-3993 or fax (317) 572-4002.

Wiley also publishes its books in a variety of electronic formats. Some content that appears in print may not be available in electronic formats. For more information about Wiley products, visit our web site at www.wiley.com.

Library of Congress Cataloging-in-Publication Data:

Suryn, Witold.
  Software quality engineering : a practitioner's approach / Witold Suryn.
      pages cm
  Includes bibliographical references and index.
  ISBN 978-1-118-59249-6 (cloth)
  1. Computer software–Quality control. I. Title.
  QA76.76.Q35S87 2014
  005.1'4–dc23

                                        2013031271

10 9 8 7 6 5 4 3 2 1

For my daughter, Gabrielle

Contents

Preface

When in the early 1980s I began my adventure with information technology, I was enthusiastic, full of ideas, and profoundly naïve. I remember one of my older colleagues at the university saying, "With the microprocessor technology you just dream out what you want to do, and it will be done so." Since then I have gone through years of using the evolving information technology and every now and then I have had to stop everything I was doing to rescue it. Quite a few times I have lost hours of work, accumulated research data, and patience. . . .

Then I began asking myself the question, "Why is all that happening?" The technology is better and better, machines are more and more powerful, yet still I don't feel comfortable with keeping my important work in one place and format only. What is missing here?

About twelve years ago I found the answer: the vision for quality of information technology and systems may be there, but it is often not engineered into the products we use.

That was the moment when the idea of this book was born. The purpose of this book is to give a concise, engineering-oriented, and practical support to IT professionals and to those who are responsible for quality of the software or system they develop; those who negotiate new systems to be developed, delivered, and installed; those who will operate and use them; and those who will maintain them. The book is also intended to serve in academia as a manual to lectures that address the subject of software or system quality.

Software and system quality engineering is discussed in this book from four different perspectives: why it is important (Chapter 1), how to make it happen (Chapter 2), application contexts (Chapter 3), and what could be done to increase trust in contemporary software and systems (Chapter 4). Every chapter offers both a layer of theoretical introduction required to correctly grasp its content and a practical part that offers hands-on recommendations.

The effective use of this book depends on the reader's level of familiarity with the subject of software and systems quality. For the readers who possess practical knowledge of software and systems quality-related standards (ISO, IEEE), a considerable part of theoretical introduction may be deemed unnecessary. For the beginners or those who want to reorient their practices toward disciplined, standards-based approaches to engineering quality into software or a system, following the path of theory to practice is recommended. Finally, the practitioners who feel very comfortable with quality engineering matter may even go directly to Chapter 2, as it offers a lot of support in terms of practical identification, definition, and execution of engineering "to-dos" required in the process of developing a system or software that possesses both functionalities *and* quality.

Witold Suryn

Chapter 1

Why Software Quality Engineering?

Quality has become a critical attribute of software products as its absence produces financial, health, and sometimes life losses. At the same time the definition, or scope, of the domain of software quality has evolved continuously from a somewhat technical perspective to a perspective that embraces human aspects such as usability and satisfaction.

An increasing business-related recognition of the importance of software quality has also made software engineering's "center of gravity" shift from *creating an engineering solution* toward *satisfying the stakeholders*. Such a shift very clearly reflects the trend within the community of stakeholders who more and more often say: "I do not want to know about *bits and bytes*. I want a solution that satisfies my needs." The critical word here is "satisfaction," for it covers both functional and quality perception of the software solution being used.

Development organizations confronted with such an approach are, in general, not entirely prepared to deal with it even if their engineers are adequately educated. Moreover, if the education is there, it is quite often acquired through experience rather than a regular educational process, as the software engineering curricula being offered, with few exceptions [1], do not emphasize the importance of teaching software quality engineering.

One of practical responses to such a situation was the development of Software Engineering Body of Knowledge (SWEBOK) [2]. SWEBOK seeks to provide the knowledge that allows universities to build such educational programs that will allow producing professionals able to stay abreast of the fast-moving industry, but it also adds a scientific and innovative component to *best practices*. The continuation of this approach is this book.

So let's ask the question, "why software quality engineering?" as three partial questions:

Software Quality Engineering: A Practitioner's Approach, First Edition. Witold Suryn.
© 2014 the Institute of Electrical and Electronics Engineers, Inc.
Published 2014 by John Wiley & Sons, Inc.

- *Why software?* Because in contemporary social life software, systems and services rendered by software are omnipresent, beginning with the watches we wear, ending with nuclear electricity plants or spaceships.
- *Why quality?* Because if these instances of software work without the required quality we may be late, dead, or lost in space.
- *Why engineering?* As in every technical domain, it is engineering that transforms ideas into products, it is the verified and validated set of "to-dos" that help develop the product that not only has required functionalities but also executes them correctly.

To make this picture complete, another question should be asked: *why at all?* There is in fact only one reason: the user. Despite decades of evolution of information technology and its tools, the user still faces risky, unreliable, and quite often unintelligent products that far too often waste his or her time or money, and wear off his or her patience. So quality engineering applied to software, systems, and related services is intended to assist developers in building good, intelligent, and reliable products; to help users request and verify their quality needs; and for those who want to use software as easily as they use a dishwasher, to shield against faulty products and unprofessional suppliers.

1.1 SOFTWARE QUALITY IN THE REAL WORLD

For the users, a software product more and more often corresponds to a black box that must effectively support their business processes. As a consequence of this natural approach, business needs become a driving force of quality software product development and a stakeholder moves to the position of a car buyer and user rather than an involuntary expert in software engineering. And what he or she perceives at the end corresponds to expressed satisfaction at using a software product that possesses *both* required functionalities and required quality. When one of them is missing, a painful process of improvements and negotiations takes place to often end by changing the supplier and replacing the product with one that is *mature* enough do its job well on both accounts.

What exactly constitutes the quality of a product is often the subject of hot debate. The reason the concept of quality is so controversial is that there is no common agreement on what it means. For some it is "degree to which a set of inherent characteristics fulfills requirements" [3], whereas for others it can be synonymous with "customer value," or even "defect levels" [4]. A possible explanation as to why any of these definitions could not win a consensus is that they generally do not recognize different perspectives of quality, such as for instance the five proposed by Kitchenham and Pfleeger [5]:

- The transcendental perspective deals with the metaphysical aspect of quality. In this view of quality, it is "something toward which we strive as an ideal, but may never implement completely."

- The user perspective is concerned with the appropriateness of the product for a given context of use.

- The manufacturing perspective represents quality as conformance to requirements. This aspect of quality is stressed by standards such as ISO 9001 [6] or models such as the Capability Maturity Model [7].

- The product perspective implies that quality can be appreciated by measuring the inherent characteristics of the product.

- The final perspective of quality is value-based. This perspective recognizes that the different perspectives of quality may have a different importance, or value, to various stakeholders.

One could argue that in a world where conformance to ISO and IEEE standards is increasingly present in contractual agreements and used as a marketing tool, all the perspectives of quality are subordinate to the manufacturing view. This predominance of the manufacturing view in software engineering can be traced back to the 1960s, when the U.S. Department of Defense and IBM gave birth to Software Quality Assurance [8]. This has led to the belief that adherence to a development process, as in manufacturing, will lead to a quality product. The corollary to this belief is that process improvement will lead to improved product quality.

This opinion is not shared unanimously, as some parts of both industry and academia find it inaccurate or at least flawed. For example, G. Dromey states:

> The flaw in this approach [that you need a quality process to produce a quality product] is that the emphasis on process usually comes at the expense of constructing, refining, and using adequate product quality models [9].

Kitchenham and Pfleeger reinforce this opinion by stating:

> There is little evidence that conformance to process standards guarantees good products. In fact, the critics of this view suggest that process standards guarantee only uniformity of output [5].

Furthermore, data available from Agile [4] projects show that high quality is attainable without following a manufacturing-like approach.

However, some studies conducted at Raytheon [10] and Motorola [11] showed that there is indeed a correlation between the maturity level of an organization as measured by the Capability Maturity Model (CMM) and the quality of the resulting product. These studies provide data on how a higher maturity level (as measured by the CMM) can lead to:

- Improved error/defect density (i.e., the error/defect density lowers as maturity improves)
- Lower error rate
- Lower cycle time (time to complete parts of the lifecycle)
- Better estimation capability.

From these results, one could conclude the quality can be improved by following a mature process. Studies of the development of lifecycle models presented by Georgiadou [12] indicate that the maturity of the development process is reflected by the emphasis and allocation of testing and other quality assurance activities. The study demonstrated that the more mature the process and its underlying life cycle model, the earlier the identification of errors in the deliverables. However, these measured improvements are directly related to the manufacturing perspective of quality. Therefore, such quality improvement efforts fail to address the other perspectives of quality. This might be one of the reasons for the perception of the "quality problem" as one of the main failings of the software engineering industry. Furthermore, studies show that improvement efforts rooted in the manufacturing perspective of quality are difficult to scale down to smaller projects and/or smaller teams [13, 14]. Indeed, rather than being scaled down in smaller projects, these practices tend to be not performed at all.

Over recent years, researchers have proposed new approaches and models that try to encompass more perspectives of quality than just the manufacturing view. Geoff Dromey [9, 15] proposed such a model in which the quality of the end product is directly related to the quality of the artifacts that are a by-product of the process being followed. The reasoning is that if quality artifacts are correctly designed and produced throughout the life cycle, then the end product shall manifest attributes of good quality. This approach can clearly be linked to the product perspective of quality with elements from the manufacturing view. This is certainly a step from the manufacturing-only approach, but it fails to view the engineering of quality as a process that covers all the perspectives of quality. In Pfleeger and Atlee [16], the reader can find valid arguments against approaches that focus only on the product perspective of quality:

> This view [the product view] is the one often advocated by software metrics experts; they assume that good internal quality indicators will lead to good external ones, such as reliability and maintainability. However, more research is needed to verify these assumptions and to determine which aspects of quality affect the actual product's use.

All of this may be true to a certain extent, but what ultimately counts is a customer's *yes* said after the delivery is finalized.

Another absolutely natural trend observable within the "population of IT customers" is the desire to be properly served without having to become proficient in information technology. A customer just wants to buy, learn how to use, and then simply use a software product, just as he or she does with a car or a TV. This boils down to an extended (or shall we just say "professional and mature") responsibility of a software supplier, who now has to know not only what the customer is able to express, but also what the customer does not know that he or she knows. And then, when all questions are asked and answered, the supplier must continue on his or her way until the product is built and delivered to the customer's satisfaction.

Similarly to mathematics, the most important part of software and software quality engineering is to understand the problem. Whatever comes after is the result

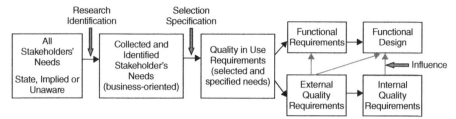

Figure 1.1   From "stated, implied, and unaware" needs to fully defined software product (based on personal communication of M. Azuma).

of knowledge applied to this understanding and, if we make an assumption that such knowledge exists, the final outcome makes the "executable form" of what was understood. The graveness of this statement is expressed by different kinds of statistics showing billion-dollar losses resulting from bad or incomplete understanding of the problem called a software product (a simple search on Google brings up thousands of hits on this subject). In case of software quality, the situation is even more dire, as the primary source of information, a customer, is usually able to at least signal his or her "functional" needs, but in the majority of situations is not knowledgeable enough to identify or discuss in precise terms the quality requested from the product under discussion. When it comes then to analyzing why something bad happened, customers blame suppliers (which is understandable) but the suppliers do not stay behind. From a purely professional point of view, one might ask: "Is that fair?" Who, between the user and the supplier, is supposed to be an expert, especially in a subject so difficult to define as quality? Should not it be the supplier who follows the process from Fig. 1.1 (with the customer having his or her "stated, implied or unaware" needs), in order to solicit, identify, and define required quality attributes and then later develop a software product that exhibits them? This question is a keynote and the main subject of this book.

1.1.1   Consumer Perspective

When a car manufacturer asks a customer about his or her opinion on the vehicle the latter uses or was using, the manufacturer, in fact, asks about an overall perception of the car in question, including both functionalities and the quality associated with them. In the case of software and even more in the case of software systems, the overall perception (or satisfaction) is heavily influenced by the verifiable existence of quality. During his many years of working in the IT industry and then teaching at a university, the author had the unique chance to ask the following question to IT professionals, students, and customers: "What would you be more inclined to accept, a system with a rich set of functionalities but with lower quality or the one with limited functionalities but with high quality?" The choice was in 99% of cases the same: the second. Interesting that the choice was identical even if the interviewed persons were from different sides of the IT market "barricade," suppliers and users. Obviously, the choice becomes less firm when suppliers return to their workstations (or we would have only high quality and bug-free software) but still, such unanimity may be interpreted as a good sign. The choice may sound "generic" as the reaction, but its real context varies for a supplier and a consumer and even inside these categories, as in the case of an individual and a corporate consumer.

1.1.1.1   Individual Consumer

In the majority of cases the individual consumer is a person with no face and no name. Unfortunately, the consumer quite often has no rights, too. The simple fact that almost every software on the planet before installation requires the acceptance of license terms that virtually free the manufacturer from any responsibility makes the existence of quality an extra effort that has in mind the good reputation of the supplier rather than the well being of the user. Currently, no known legal case initiated by an individual user against an IT giant has been won. The most common individual user reaction to a software malfunction is "reboot, and pray it works a bit longer." So, in a way, it is the user who is responsible for his or her own misery, for instead of (massively) protesting, even suing, the consumer tends to sit tight and stay quiet. There is also another perspective from which the subject may be looked at: how big is the population of faceless and disenfranchised users who experience serious troubles with individual user-targeted software? How many of us stretch the application to its limits and how many just float in the main and central current of available functionalities? From what we may observe, the latter category is dominant, or the risk of huge financial losses would motivate the suppliers better. What could (or should) be done then to assure the minimal, acceptable quality of *any* software for a Mr. John Doe? One of the emerging options is the *certification* of IT products for the individual user market. The real value of the certification is however linked to the existence of real consequences, be they financial, legal, or even only hitting someone's reputation. If the customer was inclined *not* to buy a noncertified IT product, the supplier would be motivated enough to see quality as an obligation, not as an option. The certification itself could be applied *de jure* or *de facto*, depending on the level of pressure a given society would decide to apply. One of the most important aspects of "quality for John Doe" is the identification and definition of what exactly constitutes the *minimal, acceptable quality level*. This definition would then become a pass/fail criterion used in the certification process. The very interesting beginnings of activities aiming to increase individual consumer IT products' quality can be observed in several countries such as France (Infocert [17]) and Poland (SASO [18]), or on an international level (Quality Assurance Institute [19]). Even if none of them is officially sanctioned as government requested, the market itself reacted in surprisingly positive way. In case of SASO Poland, several local IT corporations requested the possibility to begin certification process, finding it the obvious option for proving the reliability of their products and, in consequence, enhancing their market reach.

1.1.1.2 Corporate Consumer

Corporate consumers may not always have one, identifiable face but in most cases they have recognizable power to demand and obtain. The fact of being "corporate" does not limit this category of IT customers to using only big IT structures, be it a system developed on demand or an individualized suite (like the ones from SAP or Oracle). On the contrary, simpler office applications play a substantial role in corporate world even if they are not used to serve business-critical processes.

From the perspective of IT proficiency, corporate consumers may be put in two distinctive categories: pure users and user-operators. Pure users are those who make the customers of system integration organizations (SIOs) such as HP Enterprise Services (formerly Electronic Data Systems (EDS)) or Oracle. Their business philosophy is "focus on what we know how to do and pay for required specialized services." In many cases the corporate customer of an SIO not only pays for the system, its installation, and required user training, but also pays for further operation and maintenance. Such a business arrangement, popularly known as *outsourcing*, seems to be a win-win solution for all involved. In theory everybody does what he or she knows best; the user focuses on his or her core business without the burden of having his or her own IT team, and the SIO runs the system with all required professionalism and responsibility. What is the place of (in this case) system quality engineering in it?

The simple fact of separating business processes and activities from the running IT machine that supports them puts the whole quality engineering responsibility on the side of a supplier (e.g., an SIO). The customer pays, among other things, to be able to express his or her needs and to be correctly understood using principally the taxonomy natural to his or her business. In consequence, a somehow trivial statement of "I will open a new facility in Japan that has to operate 24/7" will have to be translated into a set of precise functional and quality requirements for the supporting IT system by a supplier, who further should initiate a series of technical meetings where the customer's functional and quality needs are explained, negotiated, understood, and finally agreed upon. The difficulty of this challenge gets bigger when a discussion of quality takes place. Although questions concerning functional aspects of the system are usually easily understood and answered by an IT-unfamiliar user, a question such as "what are your usability requirements?" may raise a few brows. So the supplier not only has to identify his or her customer's quality requirements, but also has to explain them, verify them, and get the fully informed customer's approval, and then engineer them into the system.

The corporate customer's supplier's responsibility does not end with installing the system, training the staff, and turning the key in the ignition. As the parties are known by name and bound by elaborate contracts, the repercussions of missing quality may be traced back and legal and financial consequences can eventually be imposed on the guilty party. If an *outsourcing* contract has been signed, the responsibility for the system and its quality stays on the side of the supplier for the length of the contract.

In case of user-operators the quality engineering problem may be slightly less difficult, as this category of corporate customers is usually "IT-savvy." The biggest

challenge in the whole process of engineering quality, the identification and definition of quality requirements, may eventually be achieved through discussions in
domain-specific language and applying domain-specific models and knowledge
(e.g., using the ISO/IEC 25000 series of standards [20]), so the road to a correct
understanding of quality needs for the given system is shorter and faster.

Then, after the installation and all required training, the system usually goes
under the operation and daily maintenance of the user's IT team, with the supplier
granting the support and warranty for a given period. Analyzing the responsibility
for quality engineering in this type of situation brings a three-phase view: in the
phase of the development and transition, it is supplier's sole responsibility; in the
phase of the user's operation covered by supplier's warranty, the responsibility is
"distributed" and creates the majority of conflicting situations because there is more
than one entity manipulating the system; and in the phase of the whole remaining
system life time the responsibility for engineering quality is entirely the user's.

One may ask, "what engineering of the quality may take place when system is
in its operation phase?" More of this subject will be discussed in Chapter 2.

1.1.2   Supplier Perspective

The supplier's ultimate justification for developing any product is the profit, usually
calculated in terms of the return on investment (ROI). It is widely known and
accepted that developing functionalities of the system or software requires appropriate budget, but it is much less publicly obvious that engineering the quality into
these functionalities costs money as well, and that it is not cheap. There is another
aspect of quality that makes it "a child of a lesser god" in eyes of a developer: too
often its presence or absence manifests itself after a considerably long time of operation. With the quality of a system or software it is like with a pair of shoes: their
"functionalities," such as shape, color, and size, can be seen immediately, but verifying their "qualities," such as real quality of materials used or comfort in use, requires
time and operation (walking a few kilometers) to be applied.

These two elements make up the basic reasoning for quality-related decisions.
In other words, if the quality is so expensive that it will make the price prohibitive
or eat up the profit, it will be reduced to a passable minimum. If, further in this
direction, its lack will not be immediately noticed or will not reach the "pain thresh-
old" of the user, it will also be reduced or even neglected. The third element in
quality-related decision making is the famous *time-to-market*, the offspring of competition. On one hand, the competition makes a supplier try to build a better product
than the other suppliers, but on the other hand, it creates a strong time pressure to
reach the market before the competitors, and that always requires compromises.
Depending on the corporate philosophy and culture of the supplier, the compromises
may be applied to both functionalities and quality or to quality only.

Financial influences are not the only ones that decide the final quality of a
software product or system. Quality requires engineering knowledge comparable to
that used in development, but this knowledge is far younger and still in dynamic

evolution. In Chapter 2, quality engineering processes and activities are discussed in detail, but to create a simple, common reference for the two following chapters, these processes are named here:

- Identification and definition of quality requirements
- Transformation of requirements into quality attributes of the future software or system
- Transformation of quality attributes into engineering "to-dos" that can be communicated to developers and further realized
- Identification and estimation of interdependencies between development and quality engineering activities
- Design of quality measurement (design of quality tests)
- Quality measurement
- Quality evaluation.

In conclusion, the supplier's perspective on quality engineering is the result of a combination of financial constraints, software quality engineering knowledge existing in the organization, and the user's tolerance to poor quality.

1.1.2.1   Off-the-Shelf Software Products

Off-the-shelf (OTS) software products are "software product(s) available for any user, at cost or not, and used without the need to conduct development activities" [21]. This definition of OTS indicates the main targeted user as the one discussed in Section 1.1.1.1, a nameless, faceless customer. The suppliers of OTS software face all quality-related dilemmas discussed previously, that is, cost, manifestation, knowledge, and time, and from what can be seen in the market, they do not deal with them too well. In their seventh decade, information technology companies still happen to deliver unreliable, poorly engineered, and sometimes surprisingly user-unfriendly products. Why?

Besides a short budget, undemanding customers, and lack of required knowledge, an OTS supplier is exposed to another challenge: a difficulty in communication with the users. A massive user is an unknown user, not reachable directly, and unfortunately also rather IT-ignorant, so not helpful in identifying missing or required quality. Then how exactly is the OTS developer supposed to build a product of required quality if he or she cannot talk to his or her customers?

There are several possible approaches to helping the developer create an OTS product of correct and appreciated quality. Some of them are:

- Collecting users' feedback through surveys
- Collecting detailed crash reports
- Sociological analysis of the targeted user groups
- Extrapolation.

In order to be effective, *collecting users' feedback* in the domain of quality requires a considerable effort of design. The questionnaire cannot be too long because the responders will become disinterested, it cannot use specialized software quality vocabulary or concepts because it may be incomprehensible, it cannot be difficult in operation because it will discourage the user, but despite of all these constraints it has to bring the required information. Additionally, in the case of OTS developers that sell their product internationally the survey has to be *localized*, which means that it not only has to be properly translated but it also has to take into consideration the cultural context of the country in which it is being run. Another element that influences the usability of the survey is its statistical value. If any important decision about developing quality attributes and budget related to it is to be made, it cannot be based on partial or invalid information; in other words, it has to come from a statistically representative group of responders. If a software product is being sold in hundreds of thousands of copies, a few hundred replies to the survey will hardly constitute a statistically valid basis for any strategic decision.

Collecting crash reports seems to be a popular tool of getting real feedback, but sometimes its undisputable value is diminished by legal and financial reality. As the author began his adventure with IT technology in late 1970s, he has seen (and survived) hundreds, if not thousands, of different crash reports, blue screens, and event logs, trying in most cases to understand the information contained in them. The reports evolved from compressed, cryptic texts unavailable to the "uninitiated" to elaborate multi-page documents describing in almost-human language every detail of the crash. To appreciate the software quality engineering-related value of these reports it is important to stress something that may seem obvious: none of them contains the information of the type "the functionality Y is missing." Crash reports are almost purely quality-related data that should help the developers make a very good *next* version/update/build of their product. Where is the problem, then?

In order to be of any use, the reports have to be transmitted to the developers. The majority of applications use fully or partially crash report generation and transmission services of the operating system they reside upon, and these services are not free of charge. A considerable number of smaller developers never receive their reports because they simply cannot afford them.

Sociological analysis of the targeted user group is the tool that through dedicated research helps identify the most important needs of this group within a predefined domain. Applying it in software quality engineering brings information about customers' needs for such characteristics as usability (ease of use, learnability, etc.) or quality in use (productivity, effectiveness, satisfaction, etc.). A good, simple illustration of such an analysis process would be the project to develop a text processor. Before making any technological and financial decisions about the quality of the new product, the developer would have to ask the following questions:

- Who is the targeted user (e.g., a mass user or a specialist)? In what country or region? In what sector of the market?

- What would be main application areas of the processor for each of the categories of the user?

- What quality attributes are associated with every identified application area of the processor?

- Are all the attributes of the same weight or they can be prioritized? In how many and what priority levels?
- Which of these attributes are mandatory and which could be done later?
- What may happen in terms of product behavior if the mandatory attributes are absent?
- What would be foreseeable reactions of the targeted user to the lack of these attributes?

After having at least these few questions thoroughly answered, the developer may begin the decision process about design, technology, and budget for quality of the new product.

Extrapolation in terms of quality is an exercise, the objective of which is to identify successful quality attributes of the new (or being improved) product through observed reactions to existing and missing quality in products launched to date. Continuing the example of a text processor, it is quite possible to observe within, for example, five consecutive versions of the product the positive response to enhanced *operability* ("operability" measures the degree to which a product or system has attributes that make it easy to operate and control [22]). So, one of the important quality attributes in a new version would be observably increased operability. Of course, nothing like *global operability* would make sense, so the developer will have to identify what functions/functionalities/services would be preferred to have increased operability. In text processing, one of the most important functions is change tracking, but this particular function in some existing processors is uncomfortable in use, unclear, unintuitive, and so on, so its operability is considerably low. The *extrapolation* in this case would indicate that to attract more customers to their product, the developers should pay particular attention to change tracking function and made it considerably more user friendly.

1.1.2.2   On-Demand Systems

This category of systems and software comprises products that require a *user-specific intervention* from a developer prior to their installation. Such an intervention can go from a simple adaptation of an office support system (a small-sized system integration effort), through a dedicated configuration of existing "suites" (such as Oracle's "E-Business" [23] or SAP's "Business One" [24]) to a complete, from-scratch development of a required solution.

No matter the size and complexity of the developer's task, from a quality engineering perspective the basic conditions are the same:

- A user is known
- Requirements are identifiable
- Required expertise should exist
- Responsibility is direct.

A *known-user* situation should at least help open direct communication channels, which in turn should allow for a professional investigation of customer's real needs of quality in the future system. As was stated in Section 1.1, the user's knowledge of quality engineering may be seriously limited, putting the majority of his or her justified quality requirements in the category of "unaware," hence the term *investigation*. Nonetheless, the developer deals here with relatively precise situation: a known user, a known or at least analyzable and definable problem, an identifiable required area of expertise, and available technology.

An *identifiable requirements* situation assumes that within an effort of creating an appropriate solution for the customer there are means to extract all relevant information necessary for further definition of correct and complete quality requirements. Keeping in mind that they may fall in all three categories differentiated by the level of difficulty in obtaining them ("stated, implied, unaware"), it can be understood that the process itself may be lengthy, demanding several iterations and a particular effort in presenting, explaining, and justifying the identified requirements. And in case of systems developed on demand, this is a sole responsibility of the developer. For more details, go to Section 2.2.1.

Required expertise simply means all expertise necessary for making quality happen in a developed system (discussed in detail in Chapter 2). What is important in real-world development situations is the *existence* of this expertise. A very popular and equally incorrect perception of quality limits it to the equivalent of "tests" or "no bugs." It is obvious that the crashless behavior of given software improves its use and increases the positive reception by a customer, but from the perspective of an overall quality, tests make only a part of the required expertise. To prove it is enough to analyze any domain-recognized software or system quality model, such as, for example, the most recent ISO/IEC 25010 [25] or even classical Boehm model [26, 27]. From this analysis it can be found that even (ideally) a bugless system may receive a low grade on quality because its productivity is not what was expected, or its use, be it business- or maintenance-related, is difficult, so slowing down the work and tiring the user. Further in this direction, the content of such a model brings the real structure of expertise required in quality engineering. If the model from ISO/IEC 25010 is taken as the reference, the required expertise spans from applying quality to architecture, design or coding, software measurement, and security mechanisms (internal/static quality), through operation and maintenance and all their related quality characteristics and attributes (external/dynamic quality), up to productivity, psychometrics, and sometimes even psychology (usability, quality in use). And to that list, the ability to design, plan, and execute required measurements and evaluate the results has to be added. It is understandable then that in industrial reality, the full coverage of such an experience would be difficult to come by, but what seems to be a real problem is that this expertise in general is too *scarce*.

One of the most important elements of on-demand development is the *direct responsibility* of the developer to his or her customer. Together with a properly constructed contract, it gives to both the customer and the supplier the tools to demand and obtain (or pursue, if need be), even if the demands are not exactly of the same nature. On one hand the imperfections in requested quality of the delivered system can be directly traced back to the supplier, properly proven and reacted upon in an appropriate legal, financial, or technical way. On the other hand, if the reasons for such a situation are rooted in, for instance, lack of cooperation from the customer, it can also be proven helping the supplier even the odds.

1.2 COST OF QUALITY

In the following chapters, the cost of quality will be discussed from two different perspectives: how to position the costs of engineering quality into software or a system in the overall project budget, and how much the consequences of missing quality may cost.

The first perspective (Section 1.2.1) analyzes the financial ramifications and challenges that the process of engineering quality into the largely understood information technology domain faces in the real, industrial world.

The second perspective (Section 1.2.2) attempts to answer a very important question: what might happen if the quality is not there?

1.2.1 Economic Ramifications of Software Quality Engineering

When undertaking the challenge of engineering quality into software, one could take into consideration a few basic facts from life:

- Everything in software engineering boils down to the user's satisfaction
- Satisfaction is conditional to the overall behavior of the system, with software products in the first place
- The behavior of any software product is perceived through features and quality
- Features and quality of software product are expressed through requirements
- Any behavior-related requirement for software product may only be realized through code.

Having these points in mind, let us open the discussion about financial ramifications of engineering quality into software or system with the following statement: *In most development projects, functionality and quality are natural enemies.*

Is this really true? Unfortunately for all IT users, yes. There are in fact very rare situations where the project budget is open; in all other cases, the budget defines the battlefield where functionality and quality fight for an upper hand (Fig. 1.2).

As shown in Fig. 1.3, function–quality–cost (FQC) economic perspectives are merciless: no matter how big the budget is, there always will be competition between features and quality.

It translates into a financially valid fact illustrated in Fig. 1.4, implementing features and quality costs, so for a constant budget (C) more features (af) means less quality (bq). And the opposite is also true, however it is much more rare.

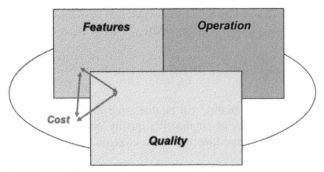

Figure 1.2   Functionality–quality battlefield.

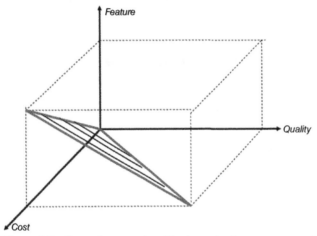

Figure 1.3   Economic perspective of implementing features versus quality (FQC).

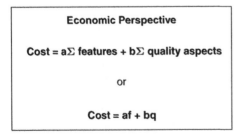

Figure 1.4   Theoretical model of financial competition between features and quality (FQC).
a, b = investment levels; f = features; q = quality aspects.

Economic Perspective

Cost = a_0f_0 + aΣ features + bΣ quality aspects

or

Cost = a_0f_0 + af + bq

Figure 1.5   Corrected model of financial competition between features and quality (FQC). a_0 = initial investment level; f_0 = initial set of features; a, b = investment levels; f = features; q = quality aspects.

The analysis of the model presented in Fig. 1.4 will immediately show that such a model, even if mathematically correct, is in fact purely theoretical. One can imagine a software product that will have features (their quantity is of no importance here) associated with the appropriate level of investment (af $\neq$ 0), but being developed with no regard to quality (bq = 0). It is however much more difficult to imagine a product having no features (af = 0), but exhibiting certain quality (bq $\neq$ 0). To correct this unrealistic representation the model has to take into account the fact that a software product that does not have at least a minimal, initial set of features does not exist. In the corrected model (Fig. 1.5), this initial set of features is represented by a_0f_0.

It is now easy to understand why in projects of a *predefined* budget, quality and functionality are enemies. And it is even easier to foresee the winner. From what can be observed in the market of software products, features continuously win, even if such victories quite often prove short-sighted. The first positive impressions based on functional richness quickly turn into disappointment or rage when the software starts producing "blue screens."

So is a software quality engineer on a by-default-lost position? Well, such a position surely is not an easy or a comfortable one, but it is still manageable and gives chances of success, if only some thoughts from the following were taken into consideration:

- From the very beginning, negotiate functional requirements with quality requirements in mind. "Later" may be too late!
- Evaluate the list of features against the budget as soon as possible. This will be your first indication about a level of possible quality, and your first argument in renegotiating the FQC proportions.
- Any functionality has its quality counterpart. Find it!
- The quality counterpart may require development or any other form of "expenditures." Take it into account when evaluating the project.
- Analyze well the existing FQC. If the quality part is considerably low, the project may quickly run into a high-risk scenario.

- A new functionality may kill the overall quality of the product, so negotiate carefully.
- A new quality requirement rarely or never harms the product.

The economic ramifications discussed in this chapter represent the point of view related to a development process and effort and as such can be considered as *internal*. The *external* ramifications attempt to analyze financial aspects of engineering quality into software in its broader, social context, also known as the *cost of missing quality*.

1.2.2   Cost of Missing Quality

The fact that IT systems are essential for the majority of tasks in human society raises a question, very important to both IT users and IT suppliers: What are the consequences of missing quality of an IT system in active use?

Every system has to make compromises in several areas and quality attributes are no exception. Different systems are subjected to different risks as they have specific quality attributes, which usually are different from one system to the other. In the ideal world, every quality attribute would be at the highest level for every system, but in practice this is not possible. As the application areas of IT systems are diversified, decisions must be made regarding which quality attributes should be given what priority in terms of the possible impacts to this area. Also, for the same reason, the cost of missing quality is different from one application area to another.

To analyze the costs of missing quality, the first helping step is to categorize the IT system in question, as within every category there are quality attributes specific or "most valuable" to it. In real-life cases, such a basic analysis should be but the beginning of a much more exhaustive process, where an impact of the absence of each application area-related quality attribute of the system has to be identified and evaluated.

The objective of the evaluation is to demonstrate the consequences of missing quality to the decision makers within an organization and, by doing so, to help them make the correct technical and budgetary decisions and prioritize the quality attributes for a system.

1.2.2.1   Cost Analysis-Based Approach

The missing quality cost (MQC) is translated into an impact on people and organizations, relative to the operation domain of the IT system. In this chapter, the MQC is analyzed applying Eppler and Helfert principles [28] with costs classified in two categories: direct and indirect.

Direct costs are directly linked to missing quality. They consist of the effects that are observable immediately after unfortunate events happen. Examples of direct costs are:

- Compensation for damages
- Physical injury and related compensations.

Indirect costs are difficult to calculate, as they may not be visibly linked to missing quality. Consequently, it is often difficult to identify them and they may remain hidden for a long time or even never discovered. Some examples of indirect costs are:

- Lost reputation or market position
- Wrong decisions or actions
- Lost investment.

1.2.2.2 Impact Analysis-Based Approach

Missing an essential quality attribute in software usually costs both the customer and the supplier, however not necessarily in equal proportions. The customer can lose data or his or her business or even, in the worst case, be exposed to physical injuries to the extent of death. Other, less dramatic impacts may include the costs linked to technical support and the costs of wasted time in investigating the source of problems. In addition, the customer may also lose his or her credibility if, due to too-low quality of his or her IT system, he or she cannot meet his or her commitments toward customers.

The cost to the supplier is most often of a different nature than the cost to the client, but there are significant impacts as well. For example, the costs of technical support can be very high due to the number of clients requesting it. Other costs include handling a large number of customer complaints, development costs to fix bugs, and the costs of supporting multiple version of the same product. Finally, the supplier may be also be pursued by the law, or forced to pay penalties to the limits of bankruptcy or loss of the market.

1.2.2.3 Risk Analysis-Based Approach

Risk analysis is an essential tool in determining the MQC, as the cost itself is usually linked to an event that could (or should) happen as the consequence of missing quality. Moreover, as the place and time of the events related to missing quality may sometimes be difficult to determine, one of the better methods for evaluation of the cost of missing quality is the classical risk analysis approach.

The risk is characterized by its probability p (where $0 < p < 1$), and impact L, also known as the potential loss (where L represents a quantity in measurable units, such as currency) [29].

Risk exposure (*RE*) is the product of the risk probability and its potential loss. This simple approach is further used when individual categories of IT systems are analyzed:

$$RE = p * L$$

Both probability p and impact L are strongly related to the level of criticality of the analyzed IT system. The most broadly known scale of the criticality in IT domain is the standardized IT system criticality levels schema published in the IEEE Standard for Software Verification and Validation [30]. The levels are:

Level A (Catastrophic)

- Continuous usage (24 hours per day)
- Irreversible environmental damages
- Loss of human lives
- Disastrous economic or social impact.

Level B (Critical)

- Continuous usage (version change interruptions)
- Environmental damages
- Serious threats to human lives
- Permanent injury or severe illness
- Important economic or social impact.

Level C (Marginal)

- Continuous usage with fix interruption periods
- Property damages
- Minor injury or illness
- Significant economic or social impact.

Level D (Negligible)

- Time-to-time usage
- Low property damages
- No risks on human lives
- Negligible economic or social impact.

1.2.2.4   Example

To illustrate the process of analyzing the consequences of missing quality, the following context based on real events (described in [31]) will be used:

- IT system application area: Nuclear power plant, system monitoring and synchronizing chemical and diagnostic data from primary (nuclear reactor) control systems.
- Quality subcharacteristic: *Recoverability* from reliability quality characteristic of ISO/IEC 25010 quality model [25].

Let's further imagine that the objective of this analysis is to convince the decision makers that much more money has to be invested into quality in general and *recoverability* in particular.

The process in simple steps could go in the following manner:

Step 1: Identify the system behavior related to the targeted quality subcharacteristic or attribute. *Recoverability* represents the level of the ability of the system to correctly recover from a serious disruption (be it a crash, an unscheduled shutdown, or even a not entirely successful update).

Step 2: Identify the criticality level of the system. The important question in this step would be: What may happen when the system that monitors and synchronizes sensitive chemical and diagnostic data from reactors recovers incorrectly? This question invokes a few more detailed questions, such as:

- What can be lost?
- What can be corrupted?
- What may happen if data or system states are corrupted (wrong)?
- What may happen if data or system states are lost?

It would be prudent to answer these questions applying the method of the worst-case scenario. In the case of the real events described in Reference 31, the corrupted (reset) data forced "safety systems to errantly interpret the lack of data as a drop in water reservoirs that cool the plant's radioactive nuclear fuel rods. As a result, automated safety systems at the plant triggered a shutdown." And this outcome can be considered very positive. In the worst-case scenario, the automated safety systems could interpret the wrong data in the opposite way (as a water overflow) and let the rods eventually melt down, causing a real disaster.

So what would be the criticality level of the analyzed system? It is not a system that directly controls the reactors but it should exhibit continuous usage capacity (with only version change interruptions), and it surely can invoke environmental damages, create serious threats to human lives, or important economic or social impact. So perhaps Level B? But what if the previously mentioned worst-case scenario should happen? The high level *recoverability* of this system could help avoid eventual further negative consequences leading to a disaster by not sending the confusing data to systems that directly control the reactors. So perhaps Level A? This decision may be taken either from the perspective of required financial efforts (so most probably Level B) or social and environmental consciousness and responsibility (so Level A), but whatever it will be, it requires a solid justification.

Step 3: Risk analysis. In this step the probability p, impact L, and risk exposure RE should be estimated in order to create information required in Step 4, cost estimation. The probability of the occurrence of the negative events related to a low level of system recoverability can be obtained through active measurements, accumulated historical data, or even observed trends in the system's behavior. In an ideal situation, the analyzed system would be disconnected from active operation and undergo a series of experiments with controlled disruptions and measured outcomes. The probability p would be calculated as the ratio between the number of experiments that created corrupted data after the recovery and the number of all experiments. Of course, information obtained in such a way would be coarse, as not every corruption of data would automatically lead to melting of radioactive rods, but it would be a solid indicator nonetheless. In real life, such an indicator can be obtained by monitoring the system behavior over a given time period and calculating the ratio between disruptions that ended with corrupted data and all disruptions that took place. To perform a precise risk analysis the probability p should be, however, calculated separately for each important category of impacts, such as what percentage of data corruption after recovery would provoke an event of false cooling water overflow indication.

Impact L has partially been analyzed in Step 2. In Step 3, the set of most important impacts should be chosen and linked to their respective probabilities. To calculate the risk exposure RE, both global and individual per impact, each impact should be translated into its mathematical representation, in its most trivial form, money. Then a simple multiplication $p \times L$ will give the values of risk exposure RE necessary for the cost analysis performed in Step 4.

Step 4: Cost analysis. The RE values obtained in Step 3 are just dry numbers that do not represent the totality of costs associated with the absence of an identified quality attribute. They may be interpreted as direct or immediate costs but the full cost analysis has to take into consideration also indirect costs, nonmonetary costs, the risk context, and, last but not least, the cost of required improvements/modifications of the system that would remedy the problem. To better explain this notion, let's take the following hypothesis: the impact of melting the rods in one of the nuclear reactors would be a (sure) destruction of the environment in the radius of 50 miles for next 70 years, a (probable) loss of human lives, and a (sure) economical disaster to the surrounding community, but the probability of it all happening as a cause of low recoverability of the system is a small but firm 1.5%. At the same time, remedying the problem would require a considerable investment (quite often the case where the legacy systems are mixed with newer generation ones). Even if everything from the preceding list capable of being transformed into monetary value was transformed so, the resulting RE would be probably relatively low, plus an extra investment required to better the existing system as the counterargument; but should it be ignored?

Step 5: Convincing the decision makers. Imagine the following exposé of yours:

Ladies and Gentlemen,
The recent analysis of our system monitoring and synchronizing chemical and diagnostic data from primary (nuclear reactor) control systems shows that its quality, in particular its recoverability, is insufficient and requires immediate intervention.

This intervention will require $X of investment and Y months of work of our (our supplier's) IT team.

The following are the data: during last N months the system went into the recovery state M times with (for example) 30% of occurrences of corrupted, after-recovery data. (For example) 1.5% of these occurrences are related to the reactor core cooling water control. We estimated the impact of possible overheating of the rods as a (sure) destruction of environment in the radius of 50 miles for next 70 years, a (probable) loss of human lives, and a (sure) economical disaster to the community around. The rough estimation of RE is $R but the overall cost, should this disaster happen, is much greater for the community, for the environment, and for our organization (insert here the list of nonfinancial consequences).

Taking this information into consideration, please grant the resources required to improve the actual situation.

The above exposé is just an example or even a template that can easily be reused in most *negative-motivation* cases of "what we lose if we do not do it" type.

Another option is a *positive-motivation* approach, or "what we gain if we do it" philosophy. The general methodology is the same, but instead of counting the possible losses, the process focuses on gains that the addition of a missing quality attribute or improvement of an existing one may bring to the system and in consequence to its creators, its users, and possibly to environment.

1.2.3 Some Important Quality Characteristics of Chosen Categories of IT Systems

In the report published in Reference 32, the authors proposed the taxonomy of most popular IT systems distributing them into four categories and eight subcategories (see Table 1.1). The discussion presented further in this chapter is based on this taxonomy.

1.2.3.1 Decision Support Systems
The main goal of decision support systems, as their name implies, is to help organizations and individuals in the process of decision making. Decision support systems usually combine data from different sources with sets of rules for analyzing them and, like all software, are subject to a set of common risks associated with the nature of software, but also possess several challenges of their own. A considerable percentage of decision support systems depend on external data sources, hence they are particularly sensitive to the quality of the data they receive to process. Another important issue that the decision support systems face are incorrect analysis algorithms.

In consequence, the important quality subcharacteristics found representative for decision support systems are *accuracy*, *analyzability*, and *suitability* [32]. These

Table 1.1   IT Systems Taxonomy

Information System Categories	Information System Subcategories
Transaction processing systems	Transactional applications systems
	Financial applications systems
Computer-based communication systems	Telecommunication
	Network management
Management information systems	Management information systems
	Information management systems
Expert systems	Decision support systems
	Industrial support (control) systems

three subcharacteristics may constitute the starting point for further analysis of quality required in a particular realization of a decision support system.

1.2.3.2 Industrial Support (Control) Systems

Industrial support (control) systems (ICSs) collect and process information related to industrial processes. A typical ICS consists of a series of sensors monitoring an industrial process and a software system to process the received data and make decisions required to properly execute the controlled process. In practice, most contemporary industrial processes use some kind of ICS. This category of systems varies from small and simple ones controlling noncritical processes to large and complex systems overseeing and running whole plants. The latter are particularly exposed to very high impacts if their ICSs do not perform as expected. Depending on the nature of the system, the impacts can be as great as irreversible damages to the environment, loss of human lives, and very high financial losses, thus, in general, it would be recommended to classify these systems at Level A of the scale presented in Section 1.2.2.

In consequence, the starting point for full quality analysis would be the quality subcharacteristics of *testability*, *accuracy*, *fault tolerance*, and *adaptability* [32].

1.2.3.3 Transaction Application System

By definition, a transaction is an individual and indivisible operation that in order to be considered completed has to be executed in its entirety. This condition is closely linked to the mechanism of *rollback*, the role of which is to get both ends of the transaction to its initial state, should the transaction fail. The most broadly known type of transaction processing is banking, where, for example, a transfer of funds from one account to the other is considered successful only when the recipient's account sends the confirmation and the sender's account receives it. In all other cases, rollback should secure the reliability of the transaction itself and force both accounts to their state from before the transaction. In more general terms, the transaction application system category consists of the systems that process information in a transactional way, ensuring that any transaction performed by them is completed or cancelled successfully. These systems also allow multiple users to manipulate the same data, usually distributed so their consistency is also of highest importance.

As the research in Reference 32 shows, the important quality characteristics found representative for transaction application systems are *functionality*, *reliability*, *usability*, and *efficiency*.

1.2.3.4 Financial Transaction Systems

A popular description of financial transaction that can be found on one of many open fora would be: "It is an event or condition under the contract between a buyer and a seller to exchange an asset for payment. In accounting, it is recognized by an entry in the books of account. It involves a change in the status of the finances of two or more businesses or individuals" [33].

The main goal of a financial transactions system is to automate the handling of financial operations. Some most popular examples of this type of systems are purchase applications, loans management systems, mortgage management systems, systems to manage bank accounts, systems to manage credit card purchases, and systems to manage debit card purchases. In all cases, quality attributes (or subcharacteristics) of accuracy, maturity, and recoverability seem to be essential. These subcharacteristics can be further folded into two main quality characteristics for the financial transaction systems: *functionality* and *reliability* [32].

1.2.3.5   Network Management Systems

Network management systems manage, administer, and monitor networks on which organizations rely to carry data from node to node. These systems have to be interoperable, reliable, and tolerant to faults, as most of their users cannot afford to have communications seriously disrupted [34]. According to the research presented in Reference 32, the most important quality factors for this type of systems are *fault tolerance*, *interoperability*, and *operability*.

1.2.3.6   Telecommunication Systems

Telecommunication systems are the backbone of the telecom operator's business model. They use huge infrastructures such as telecommunication towers, satellites, and undersea cables and regroup the operation, administration, maintenance, and provisioning functions. These management functions executed by large IT structures provide systems or networks with fault indication, performance monitoring, security management, diagnostic functions on traffic, configuration, billing, and user data provisioning. What has also to be taken into account is the fact that the existing telecommunication technology varies from older systems embedded in various types of hardware to modern, fully *soft* installations, and all of them have to cooperate and coexist in a productive manner. Quality characteristics that address these concerns would be: *functionality*, *reliability*, *usability*, and *efficiency* [32].

1.2.3.7   Management Information Systems

Management information systems are primarily used by managers and business domain experts to make business forecasts and decisions. As these users usually have a limited IT proficiency, the ease of use is a key efficiency feature. From a business use perspective, management information systems provide data necessary for strategic decision making, with services such as:

- Generating financial statements, as well as inventory reports or sales status reports.
- Answering managers' questions by offering different decision scenarios with their results.
- Supporting human resources-related decision making.
- Providing information for analysis and budget planning.
- Facilitating audits by giving complete audit trail.

The quality subcharacteristics important for these services are: *functionality*, *usability*, and *maintainability* [32].

1.2.3.8   Information Management Systems

"Information management system" is a broad term that describes a multitude of systems of which the main objective is to manage information. Some of the subcategories of these types of systems are content management systems, document management systems, digital asset management systems, or geographic information systems [35].

The common functionality of such systems is the ability to retrieve, store, and manipulate information. What is interesting is the fact that in many cases the critical risk factor that affects these systems is not related to the system infrastructure itself, but to the information they manage. In consequence, as found in Reference 32, the most important quality factors for this type of systems could be considered *security*, *operability*, *accuracy*, and *changeability*.

1.2.3.9   Practical Observations

One of interesting observations made in the course of analyzing the relationship between the category of an IT system and quality characteristics important for its use was the finding that missing "crown" quality attributes that characterize this category are not always the ones that make it fail. As some case studies have showed (see the Appendix, Case 11), the lack of a quality attribute off the main list (obviously wrongly seen as "minor") sometimes may have a bigger impact than one considered "main." This is why the idea discussed already in Section 1.2.2 will be repeated: In real-life cases, the analysis of typical-for-the-system quality attributes should be but the beginning of a much more exhaustive process, where an impact of the absence of each application area-related quality attribute of the system has to be identified and evaluated.

And finally, ensuring quality in software enhances operational effectiveness and helps accomplish strategic objectives of the organization:

- Developing modern, reliable, and environment-friendly solutions
- Keeping costs and spending low
- Keeping customers and adding new ones by giving a good service that meets and exceeds expectations.

If these goals are to be effectively achieved, software quality must make significant progress in terms of its recognition and importance in the business world, where the costs associated with missing quality should be treated in more explicit, prominent, and measurable ways.

1.3   QUALITY OF A SOFTWARE PRODUCT AS AN INDICATOR OF MATURITY

Is quality really an indicator of maturity? It is not an ultimate and always true evaluation, but in most cases quality goes with maturity. Young, immature companies usually cannot afford developing more than just a set of attractive functionalities, whereas mature organizations can develop quality too, so in this sense the level of quality observed in a software product is an indicator of the level of maturity of its developer. When evaluating the maturity of a software development organization, one can apply sophisticated methods and models such as CCMI, SPICE, or ISO 9000 and still arrive at conclusions that may not entirely reflect the reality. All the best processes will not replace the tangible indicators of the real maturity: functionalities and quality of the product. One may even say that because functionalities are always in a product and quality is only sometimes present, quality is a more restrictive indicator.

1.3.1 CMM/CMMI

The Capability Maturity Model (CMM) was born in 1990 as result of the research effort conducted by specialists from Software Engineering Institute (SEI) of Carnegie Mellon University [7]. Its next version, Capability Maturity Model Integration (CMMI^{SM}), is known in the industry as a best practices model. It combines practices of systems engineering (SE), software engineering (SWE), integrated process and product development (IPPD), and supplier sourcing (SS) disciplines. The CMMI is mostly used to "provide guidance for an organization to improve its processes and ability to manage development, acquisition, and maintenance of products and services." The CMMI (Table 1.2) was conceived to allow organizations to rely on a single model to evaluate their maturity and process capability, establish priorities for improvements, and help them improve their practices.

The CMMI is available for various combinations of disciplines in two representations: "staged" and "continuous." The model is divided into process areas (PA), each of which contains a set of generic and specific practices (Fig. 1.6) that through their existence (or lack) may manifest the maturity of an organization. In search for references to quality in CMM/CMMI manual one immediately finds the following announcement: "[In CMM] the phrase 'quality and process-performance objectives' covers objectives and requirements for product quality, service quality, and process performance."

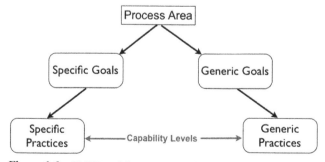

Figure 1.6   CMMI model components (adapted from [7]).

Table 1.2   Capability Maturity Model of SEI (adapted from [7])

Maturity Levels	Process Areas
5. Optimizing	Causal analysis and resolution
	Organizational innovation and deployment
4. Quantitatively managed	Quantitative project management
	Organizational process performance
3. Defined	Organizational environment for integration
	Decision analysis and resolution
	Integrated supplier management
	Integrated teaming
	Risk management
	Integrated project management for IPPD
	Organizational training
	Organizational process definition
	Organizational Process Focus
	Validation
	Verification
	Product Integration
	Technical Solution
	Requirements Development
2. Managed	Configuration management
	Process and product quality assurance
	Measurement and analysis
	Supplier agreement management
	Project monitoring and control
	Project planning
	Requirements management
1. Initial	None

More detailed analysis will yield more than 400 references to "quality" within the CMM/CMMI manual, but all of them will bear the notion of *a process* that in one way or another should *help* create a software product of quality. A quick illustration of the presence of the subject of quality within the maturity levels could look as follows:

- Level 1: None
- Level 2: Specific objectives for the performance of the process (e.g., quality, time scale, cycle time, and resource usage)
- Level 3: Same as Level 2
- Level 4: The quality and process performance are understood in statistical terms and are managed throughout the life of the process

- Level 5: Select and systematically deploy process and technology improvements that contribute to meeting established quality and process-performance objectives.

What is then the link between the maturity of an organization and quality of its products? First and foremost: it is *nonautomatic*. The organization may have all best processes in place, be continuously certified ISO 9000, and still manufacture products that will not survive a day. The level of maturity could be compared to the knowledge of a battlefield—the deeper that knowledge is, the higher are the chances of victory. But they are still only chances, not certainty.

1.3.2 SPICE ISO 15504

Software Process Improvement and Capability Determination (SPICE) is an international initiative to support the development of an International Standard for Software Process Assessment [36]. The first working draft was developed in June 1995, with the release to ISO/IEC for the normal process for development of international standards. In 1998 the documents were published as ISO/IEC TR 15504:1998—Software Process Assessment. As of now, SPICE in its ISO/IEC 15504 international standard form has ten parts, the publishing of which spans over the last decade:

- Part 1: Concepts and vocabulary
- Part 2: Performing an assessment
- Part 3: Guidance on performing an assessment
- Part 4: Guidance on use for process improvement and process capability determination
- Part 5: An exemplar process assessment model
- Part 6: An exemplar system life cycle process assessment model
- Part 7: Assessment of organizational maturity
- Part 8: An exemplar process assessment model for IT service management
- Part 9: Target process profiles
- Part 10: Safety extension

SPICE, or ISO/IEC 15504 series of standards, provides a framework for the assessment of processes. This framework can be used by organizations involved in planning, managing, monitoring, controlling, and improving the acquisition, supply, development, operation, evolution, and support of products/services. Process assessment examines the processes used by an organization to determine whether they are effective in achieving their goals. The results may be used to drive process improvement activities or process capability determination by analyzing the results in the context of the organization's business needs, identifying strengths, weaknesses, and risks inherent in the processes.

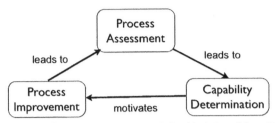

Figure 1.7   Process assessment relationship (adapted from [36]).

SPICE provides a structured approach for the assessment of processes for the following purposes:

- By or on behalf of an organization with the objective of understanding the state of its own processes for process improvement

- By or on behalf of an organization with the objective of determining the suitability of its own processes for a particular requirement or class of requirements

- By or on behalf of one organization with the objective of determining the suitability of another organization's processes for a particular contract or class of contracts.

The framework for process assessment proposed in SPICE is intended to facilitate self-assessment, provide a basis for use in process improvement and capability determination, take into account the context in which the assessed process is implemented, produce a process rating, address the ability of the process to achieve its purpose, be used across all application domains and sizes of organization, and give the chance for an objective benchmark between organizations.

Through this, the organization is expected to become a capable organization that maximizes its responsiveness to customer and market requirements, minimizes the full life cycle costs of its products, and as a result maximizes end-user satisfaction.

As can be seen in Fig. 1.7, SPICE has two principal contexts for its use: process improvement and capability determination. The relationship between SPICE, process maturity, and software product quality is indirect and bears features such as these indicated when CMM/CMMI was discussed. Maturity and efficiency of processes existing in an organization that develops software make without doubt very important foundations for the quality of product, but here the influence ends. The rest must be done by software engineers who know how to put quality into what they are about to produce.

1.3.3 SWEBOK

The purpose of the Guide to Software Engineering Body of Knowledge, called further SWEBOK, is "to provide a consensually-validated characterization of the

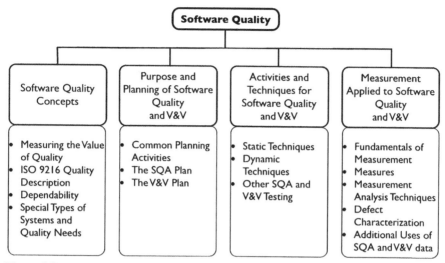

Figure 1.8   Breakdown of topics for software quality (adapted from [2]).

bounds of the software engineering discipline and to provide a topical access to the Body of Knowledge supporting that discipline." To address this objective, the 2004 edition of Body of Knowledge is subdivided into ten knowledge areas (KA) and "the descriptions of the KAs are designed to discriminate among the various important concepts, permitting readers to find their way quickly to subjects of interest" [2].

Among these ten knowledge areas, a KA dedicated to software quality has its distinctive place. Like all other KAs within SWEBOK, the software quality subject is broken down and then discussed in individual topics (15) (Fig. 1.8) grouped in four sections:

- Software Quality Concepts (SQC)
- Purpose and Planning of SQA and V&V (P&P)
- Activities and techniques for SQA and V&V (A&T)
- Other SQA and V&V Testing (OT).

As the content of the Software Quality KA of SWEBOK is rather voluminous, it cannot be discussed to its full extent in this chapter, however, some "reader's digest" given below could help the reader identify the subjects of his or her particular interest and then further pursue them through the lecture of the full text of the guide.

In *Software Quality Concepts*, the guide discusses the issues linked to identification and management of costs related to quality (and indirectly to its lack) and modeling of quality, stresses the importance of quality in the context of dependability of software products, and points out the existence of quality perspectives other than these "classical" perspectives perceived through the lenses of ISO/IEC 9126 series of standards [37 to 40].

Purpose and Planning of SQA and V&V analyzes planning and objectives of software quality assurance (SQA) and verification and validation (V&V) processes in the context of what, when, and how quality should be achieved.

Activities and Techniques for SQA and V&V tackles practicalities of SQA and V&V execution, presenting among the others static and dynamic techniques recommended for these processes.

Measurement Applied to SQA and V&V presents basic notions of measurement theory and practice in context of software and software quality measurement.

As profound as may be the way in which SWEBOK discusses software quality, it still leaves some room for additional perspectives. One of them is the *engineering* perspective of making real quality happen (or, using simpler vocabulary, hands-on engineering interventions). This hypothesis lies at foundations of the research program conducted and published in 2006 [41] with the objective of evaluating each KA constituting SWEBOK in order to verify the level of representation of the subject of software quality engineering in this most prominent document of software engineering domain.

As part of this research, the latest version of SWEBOK had been analyzed from the perspective of the core processes constituting the practices of software quality engineering. These core processes were identified through the analysis of software life cycle processes published in the standard ISO/IEC 12207: 1995 (the 2008 version was still in redaction) [42] supported by the results of the research on software engineering principles [43] and software quality implementation models (discussed further in Section 2.3.1).

The dedicated analysis methodology developed in order to execute the research program consisted of four phases, presented Fig. 1.9:

- *Phase 1:* Analysis, validation, and, if necessary, addition of definitions of software quality engineering processes in Software Life Cycle (SLC) processes and activities identified in ISO/IEC 12207.

- *Phase 2:* Analysis, validation, adjustment (if necessary), and mapping of the set of basic processes of software engineering definitions identified in ISO/IEC 12207 with the processes and activities described in respective KAs of SWEBOK.

- *Phase 3:* Application and assessment of results of the mapping between the processes of software quality engineering identified in Phase 1 with the processes and activities described in KAs of SWEBOK (Phase 2).

- *Phase 4:* Identification and definition of applicable modifications to SWEBOK.

The results published in [41] take several pages of tables and definitions; however, some general conclusions that emerged from this research would be:

- Quality as engineering process is addressed in a limited form, to say the least

- The basic quality engineering activities such as quality requirements specification or modeling are not recognized anywhere

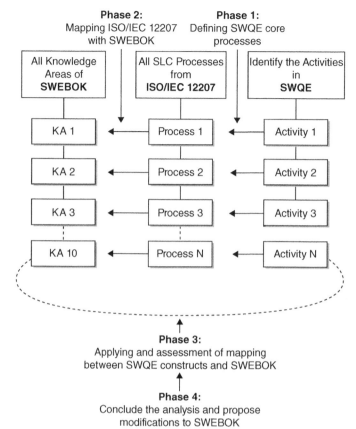

Figure 1.9   The architecture of the research methodology software quality engineering in SWEBOK [41].

- Quality testing is discussed almost only in reference to V&V processes, while in fact real evaluation of software product happens all along the life cycle

- Practical aspects of engineering quality into a software product are entirely omitted, while their appearance would be helpful at least in Software Construction KA.

Apart from a very basic conclusion about modifications that could enrich SWEBOK, one other of a more general nature comes to mind: software quality engineering, like its mother domain, software engineering, is still far from gaining stability and maturity and requires continuous research effort supported by wide cooperation with the IT industry.

The development works on SWEBOK are continued as a joint effort between the ISO/IEC JTC SC7 committee and the IEEE Computer Society, giving as the result several enhancements to its 2004 edition, including new KAs. The new edition is expected to be publicly available in 2014.

REFERENCES

1. École de technologie supérieure, education program in software quality. Montreal, Canada. Available at http://www.etsmtl.ca.
2. Abran A, Moore JW, Bourque P, Dupuis R, editors. *Guide to the Software Engineering Body of Knowledge*, 2004. Los Alamitos: IEEE Computer Society, 2004.
3. ISO 9000 Quality Management Systems—Fundamentals and Vocabulary. Geneva, Switzerland: International Organization for Standardization, 2005.
4. Highsmith J. *Agile Software Development Ecosystems*. Addison Wesley, 2002.
5. Kitchenham B, Pfleeger SL. "Software Quality: The Elusive Target." *IEEE Software* 1996; 13(1):12–21.
6. ISO 9001 Quality Management Systems—Requirements. Geneva, Switzerland: International Organization for Standardization, 2008.
7. CMMI-SE/SW/IPPD/SS 2002. CMMI Team, Capability Maturity Model Integration for Systems Engineering, Software Engineering, Integrated Product and Process Development, and Supplier Sourcing (CMMI-SE/SW/IPPD/SS), Version 1.1, Continuous Representation. Pittsburgh: Software Engineering Institute, Carnegie Mellon University, 2002.
8. Voas J. "Assuring Software Quality Assurance." *IEEE Software* 2003; 20(3):48–49.
9. Dromey RG. "Cornering the Chimera." *IEEE Software* 1996; 13(1):33–43.
10. Haley TJ. "Software Process Improvement at Raytheon." *IEEE Software* 1996; 13(6):33–41.
11. Diaz M, Sligo J. "How Software Process Improvement Helped Motorola." *IEEE Software* 1997; 17(5):75–81.
12. Georgiadou E. "Software Process and Product Improvement: A Historical Perspective." *International Journal of Cybernetics* 2003; 1(1):172–197.
13. Laitinen M. "Scaling Down Is Hard to Do." *IEEE Software* 2000; 17(5):78–80.
14. Boddie J. "Do We Ever Really Scale Down?" *IEEE Software* 2000; 17(5):79–81.
15. Dromey RG. "A Model for Software Product Quality." *IEEE Transactions on Software Engineering* 1995; 21:146–162.
16. Pfleeger SL, Atlee JM. *Software Engineering: Theory and Practice*, 4th ed. Upper Saddle River: Prentice Hall, 2009.
17. INFOCERT. http://www.infocert.org.
18. SASO. http://www.saso.org.pl.
19. Quality Assurance Institute. http://www.qaiglobalinstitute.com.
20. ISO/IEC 25000 System and Software Engineering—SQuaRE—Software Product Quality Requirements and Evaluation. Geneva, Switzerland: International Organization for Standardization, 2005–2013.
21. ISO/IEC 25051 Software Engineering—Software Product Quality Requirements and Evaluation (SQuaRE)—Requirements for Quality of Commercial Off-the-Self (COTS) Software Products and Instructions for Testing. Geneva, Switzerland: International Organization for Standardization, 2006.
22. ISO/IEC 25023 Systems and Software Engineering—Systems and Software Quality Requirements and Evaluation (SQuaRE)—Measurement of System and Software Product Quality. Geneva, Switzerland: International Organization for Standardization; document in development.
23. Oracle E-Business Suite. http://www.oracle.com/us/solutions/oos/e-business-suite/overview/index.html.

24. SAP Business Suite. http://www54.sap.com/solution/lob/finance/software/business-suite-apps-hana/index.html.

25. ISO/IEC 25010 Systems and Software Engineering—Systems and Software Quality Requirements and Evaluation (SQuaRE)—System and Software Quality Models. Geneva, Switzerland: International Organization for Standardization, 2011.

26. Selby R, editor. *Software Engineering: Barry Boehm's Lifetime Contributions to Software Development, Management and Research*. New York: Wiley/IEEE Press, 2007.

27. Boehm BW, Brown JR, Kaspar JR, Lipow ML, MacCleod G. *Characteristics of Software Quality*. New York: American Elsevier, 1978.

28. Eppler MJ, Helfert M. "A Framework for the Classification of Data Quality Costs and an Analysis of their Progression." In *International Conference on Information Quality; November 5–7, 2004*. Cambridge: Massachusetts Institute of Technology, 2004.

29. Fairley RE. *Managing and Leading Software Projects*. Hoboken, N.J.: Wiley IEEE Computer Society, 2009.

30. IEEE Standard 1012–2004. *IEEE Standard for Software Verification and Validation*. New York: IEEE Computer Society, 2004.

31. Krebs B. "Cyber Incident Blamed for Nuclear Power Plant Shutdown." *The Washington Post*, June 5, 2008.

32. Suryn W, Trudeau PO, Mazzetti C. "Information Systems and their Relationship to Quality Engineering." 17th Software Quality Management International Conference, April 6–8, 2009, Southampton, UK.

33. "Financial transaction," http://en.wikipedia.org/wiki/Financial_transaction.

34. Boutaba R, Xiao J. "Network Management: State of the Art." *The International Federation for Information Processing* 2002; 92:127–145.

35. Robertson J. "Step Two Designs: Definition of Information Management Terms." Available at http://www.steptwo.com.au/papers/cmb_definition/index.html. Accessed May 14, 2013.

36. ISO/IEC 15504 (SPICE) Information Technology—Process Assessment Series of Standards. Geneva, Switzerland: International Organization for Standardization, documents in development.

37. ISO/IEC 9126-1 Software Engineering—Product Quality—Part 1: Quality Model. Geneva, Switzerland: International Organization for Standardization, 2001.

38. ISO 9126-2 Software Engineering—Product Quality—Part 2: External Metrics. Geneva, Switzerland: International Organization for Standardization, 2003.

39. ISO 9126-3 Software Engineering—Product Quality—Part 3: Internal Metrics. Geneva, Switzerland: International Organization for Standardization, 2003.

40. ISO 9126-4 Software Engineering—Product Quality—Part 4: Quality in Use Metrics. Geneva, Switzerland: International Organization for Standardization, 2004.

41. Suryn W, Stambollian A, Dormeux JC, Bégnoche L. "Software Quality Engineering—Where to Find It in Software Engineering Body of Knowledge (SWEBOK)." 14th Software Quality Management International Conference; April 10–12, 2006, Southampton, UK.

42. ISO/IEC 12207 Information Technology—Software Life Cycle Processes. Geneva, Switzerland: International Organization for Standardization, 1995.

43. Bourque P, Dupuis R, Abran A, Moore JW, Tripp L, Wolff S. "Fundamental Principles of Software Engineering: A Journey." *Journal of Systems and Software* 2002; 62: 59–70.

Chapter 2

Software Quality Engineering: Making It Happen

Making quality happen in a real, industrial development requires organized knowledge, obtained either through years of practical experiments or in the educational process. Such knowledge, to be complete, should encompass practical approaches to software quality engineering, beginning with necessary basic concepts, then requirements, design, implementation, and V&V, finishing with managerial decisions relative to the whole process. All these subjects are discussed in following chapters.

2.1 BASIC CONCEPTS OF SOFTWARE QUALITY

In Section 1.1.1, when discussing software quality in the real world, we asked the following two questions:

- Who, between the user and the supplier, is supposed to be an expert, especially in a subject so difficult to define as quality?
- Should not it be the supplier who solicits, identifies, and defines required quality attributes (from working with the user) and then later develops a software product that exhibits them?

Among the numerous rationales for these questions, one seems to be of special importance: the basic concepts of software quality are rather unknown within the community of information technology users, and, what is much worse, are sometimes also unknown or neglected by the community of developers. It then seems appropriate to introduce the readers of this book to some basic notions required to obtain a view of the nature and objectives of software quality engineering.

Software Quality Engineering: A Practitioner's Approach, First Edition. Witold Suryn.
© 2014 the Institute of Electrical and Electronics Engineers, Inc.
Published 2014 by John Wiley & Sons, Inc.

2.1.1 Software Quality Engineering Nature and Definition

An engineering process can basically be expressed in terms of a problem and its resolution. In other words, an *engineer* is a knowledgeable person, who through his or her education supported by experience is able to understand (i.e. investigate, identify, and break down) a problem and deliver a solution that resolves it. To be an engineer means to be a problem solver, as shown in Fig. 2.1.

To be an engineer means also something else. As was once said by our friend, a Polish scientist and engineer, "an engineer is neither a profession nor a career, it is a way of thinking." This very true observation, when used in our daily practice, will differentiate creators from repeaters. In software engineering such differentiation may prevail upon the success or the failure of the project, not necessarily only in terms of technical results but also as a solution that may satisfy the user, create a new, market-leading product, or just advance the technology.

The most known definition of *engineering* is the one proposed and published by The Accreditation Board for Engineering and Technology [2]. It states: "Engineering is the profession in which a knowledge of the mathematical and natural sciences, gained by study, experience, and practice, is applied with judgment to develop ways to utilize, economically, the materials and forces of nature for the benefit of mankind."

In a smaller scale but still in a similar way, the definition of software engineering has been proposed and further published by IEEE CS in its broadly known standard IEEE 610.12 [3]:

1. The application of a systematic, disciplined, quantifiable approach to the development, operation, and maintenance of software; that is, the application of engineering to software,

2. The study of approaches as in (1).

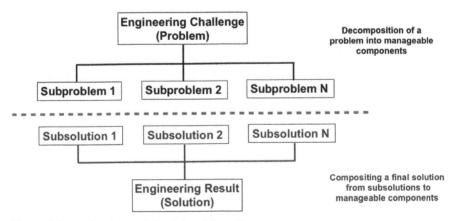

Figure 2.1 Engineering a solution (adapted from [1]).

Finally, a definition of software quality engineering that complements the one from IEEE 610.12 has been developed and proposed in [4]:

1. The application of a continuous, systematic, disciplined, quantifiable approach to the development and maintenance of quality of software products and systems; that is, the application of quality engineering to software,

2. The study of approaches as in (1).

What should be added to this definition of software quality engineering to make it something more than just a theoretical divagation is the subject of its applicability within the life cycle of the software (product or system). Among the results of the worldwide research on software engineering fundamental principles published in [5] one very important engineering idea has been identified and further recognized as the "fundamental principle candidate": "Manage quality <u>throughout the life cycle</u> as formally as possible."

This idea translates into a practical approach that is of fundamental value to building software of quality, the approach that is "known" but largely neglected within software development industry: building quality into software is an engineering effort that must be active throughout the whole life cycle of software to bring required results.

The same statement bears also the importance that directly influences the definition of software quality engineering presented earlier. To comply with the requirement of continuity, the new definition of software quality engineering shall state:

1. The application of a continuous, systematic, disciplined, quantifiable approach to the development and maintenance of quality throughout the whole life cycle of software products and systems; that is, the application of quality engineering to software,

2. The study of approaches as in (1).

In this book all further mentions of the "software quality engineering definition" will refer to the above text.

2.1.2 Objects of Software Quality Engineering

What exactly is an object of software quality engineering in the twenty-first century? Is it a collection of lines of code that should do something and should do it correctly? Or perhaps a collection of software modules that, when linked together, are able to deliver a service? Going further, one may guess that the quality should also apply to large, multipart software structures, but is that all and where is the limit? To answer this very basic question, one other must be asked: what constitutes real software (a product) that would be accepted by the buyer/user? One of the best-known definitions of such a product was published in Reference 6:

> Software is (1) instructions (computer programs) that when executed provide desired function and performance, (2) data structures that enable the programs to adequately manipulate information, and (3) documents that describe the operations and use of the programs.

In the twenty-first century this definition is still valid, but not wide enough, as it does not encompass all the richness of developed products, their actual applications, and related user expectations. The contemporary "software products" vary from simple, off-the-shelf (OTS) software to global sophisticated systems, their applications range from text processing to space flight control, and their users may represent individuals as well as international behemoths of organizations.

The notion that would better correspond to such a reality is a *system*. The *system* may be very complex or not but it contains both technical and nontechnical elements (Fig. 2.2) that offer *completeness* of what is required and should be delivered to a customer to obtain his or her satisfaction.

Based on a generic definition that could be found in most popular dictionaries, a software system can be defined as: "A collection of functionally arranged software components, related artifacts, resources and services that are organized to accomplish a predefined goal by processing information."

Either of the two representations clearly indicates that a system is a combination of software (with all its intrinsic complexity) and the additional elements required by the user to execute his or her tasks effectively, efficiently, and with satisfaction.

What is then a customer's satisfaction? Will the user be satisfied by the product that has a richness of functionalities but every now and then freezes, or produces the infamous blue screen, or just restarts uncontrollably, losing the user's data? Will this user congratulate his or her supplier if the system is stone-rigid but misses half of the requested functionalities? Will the supplier be fully paid if the system comes

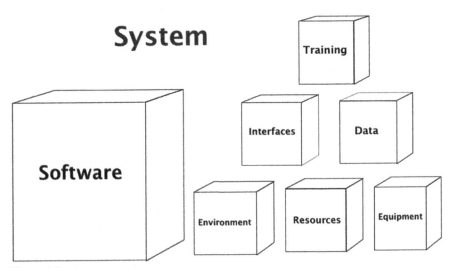

Figure 2.2 Components of a system.

without proper documentation and training? Any one of those cases will result in a seriously dissatisfied customer and a possibility of losing the market. The only situation that may create a fully satisfied client is when the system exhibits requested services complemented by appropriate quality and accompanied by good and complete documentation, professional service, and training.

If this is true and both previously presented descriptions define what constitutes a delivered product, what would be the objects of software quality engineering? To identify these objects it may prove fruitful to define the perspectives from which a software system quality may be perceived. ISO 9126-1 [7] proposes three distinctive views that correspond well to three most popular categories of stakeholders:

- Internal quality represents the perspective of the developer and maintainer (later in the life cycle of a system)
- External quality represents the perspective of the maintainer, operator, and partially of the end user (in its usability aspect)
- Quality in use represents the perspective of the end user.

These views can also be very easily linked to the phases of a generic model of the development process:

- Internal quality is crucial in construction phase
- External quality plays the biggest role in design and later, from the system tests phase until the system is decommissioned
- Quality in use should be observed in the requirements definition phase and then again from the system tests phase until the system is decommissioned.

Finally, using the same three views we can identify the "physical targets" of software quality engineering:

- Internal quality operates on code (developed or being developed) and related artifacts such as source documents, architecture, documentation, plans, and results of unitary tests
- External quality operates on running executables in so-called technical environment (operation and maintenance), related artifacts such as architecture, operation documentation, manuals, plans and results of system tests, and related services such as operation and maintenance training
- Quality in use operates on the ready product in its business environment (both emulated and real) and related artifacts such as all user manuals and services (application and usage training).

Taking all these aspects into consideration it can be then said, without the risk of serious omission, that the real object of software quality engineering is a software system with all its components, but that undergoes quality engineering appropriate to and required by the actual phase of its life cycle and corresponding to perspectives of stakeholders that participate in this phase.

2.1.3 Quality Models

Quality models present an approach to tie together different quality attributes with basic objectives to:

- Help understand how the several facets of quality contribute to the whole
- Emphasize clearly that software quality is much more than simply faults and failures
- Help identify and define quality requirements
- Help to navigate through the map of quality characteristics, subcharacteristics, and appropriate measures (measurement formulas and scales)
- Help to define an evaluation profile (what precisely should be evaluated).

Software quality engineering calls for a formal management of quality throughout the full lifecycle of software or a system. In order to support this requirement, a quality model should have the ability to support both the definition of quality requirements and their subsequent evaluation. This can be explained by referring to the manufacturing perspective of quality, which states that quality is conformance to requirements. A quality model that is to be used in the definition of quality requirements should help in both the specification of quality requirements and the evaluation of software quality.

IEEE Standard 1061–1998 [8] defines this as a top-to-bottom and bottom-to-top approach to quality:

- From a top down perspective the [quality] framework facilitates:
  - ○ establishment of quality requirements factors, by customers and managers early in a system's life cycle
  - ○ communication of the established quality factors, in terms of quality sub-factors, to the technical personnel
  - ○ identification of metrics that are related to the established quality factors and quality sub-factors.
- From a bottom up perspective the [quality] framework enables the managerial and technical personnel to obtain feedback by:
  - ○ evaluating the software products and processes at the metrics level
  - ○ analyzing the metric values to estimate and assess the quality factors.

Since early 1970s there have been continual attempts to create a valid, broadly accepted quality model. Some of the latest works in the subject propose a generic, customizable quality model (such as GEQUAMO [9]), which enables any stakeholder to construct his or her own model depending on the requirements. More recently, a survey amongst practitioners from the UK, Greece, Egypt, and Cyprus presented in Reference 10 indicated the importance placed on product quality characteristics, resulting in the proposition of enhancements to the existing quality models (such as adding two new characteristics of *extensibility* and *security* to ISO/IEC 9126 quality model).

These observations indicate the existence of disagreements, or different views, in both the research community and the industry on the subject of software quality. The goal of a quality model is, in essence, to provide an operational definition of quality. Although specific definitions have been established for given contexts, there is no consensus as to what constitutes quality in the general sense in software engineering.

From the software quality engineering perspective, for a quality model to be useful it should:

- Support the five different perspectives of quality as defined by Kitchenham and Pfleeger [11] (see Section 1.1)
- Be usable from the *top to the bottom* of the life cycle as defined by IEEE Standard 1061–1998 [8], that is, should allow for defining quality requirements and their further decomposition into appropriate quality characteristics, subcharacteristics, and measures
- Be usable from the *bottom to top* of the lifecycle as defined by IEEE Standard 1061–1998 [8], that is, should allow for required measurements and subsequent aggregation and evaluation of obtained results.

Several quality models were developed in the course of past three decades, some of them recognized mostly by the scientific community, others also gaining recognition within the industry. The most widely known models, presented further in this chapter, are those of McCall, Boehm, Dromey, ISO/IEC 9126, and ISO/IEC 25010.

2.1.3.1   McCall's Quality Model

McCall [12] introduced his quality model in 1977 (Fig. 2.3) in response to the observable need to define quality in some usable and orderly manner. In McCall's model, each quality factor on the higher level of the figure represents an aspect of quality that is not directly measurable. On the lower level are the measurable properties that can be evaluated in order to quantify the quality in terms of the factors. McCall proposes a subjective grading scheme ranging from 0 (low) to 10 (high); unfortunately, many of the metrics defined by McCall can be measured only subjectively. Furthermore, some of the factors and measurable properties, such as traceability and self-documentation, are not really definable or even meaningful at an early stage for nontechnical stakeholders. From this perspective this model does not satisfy the criteria outlined in the IEEE Standard 1061–1998 [8] for a top-to-bottom approach to quality engineering. Also, as it emphasizes the product perspective of quality to the detriment of the other perspectives, it is not entirely usable in software quality engineering according to the earlier stated requirements.

42

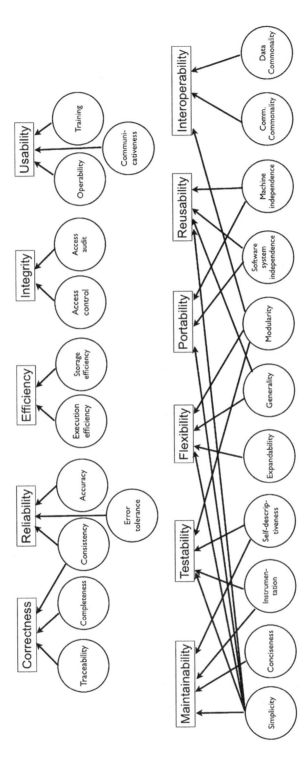

Figure 2.3 McCall's quality model (adapted from [1] and [12]).

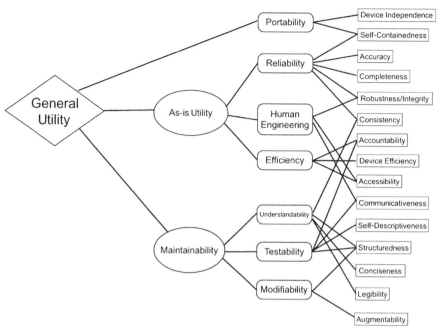

Figure 2.4   Boehm's quality model (adapted from [1] and [13]).

2.1.3.2   Boehm's Quality Model

Boehm's quality model [52] improves upon the work of McCall, however, as Fig. 2.4 shows, this quality model loosely retains the factor-measurable property arrangement.

If the semantic of McCall's model is used as a reference, the quality factors in Boehm's model can be defined as portability, reliability, efficiency, human engineering, testability, understandability, and modifiability. These factors can be decomposed into measurable properties such as device independence, accuracy, and completeness. Portability is somewhat incoherent in this classification as it acts both as a top-level component of general utility and as a factor that possesses measurable attributes.

It is interesting to note that in opposition to McCall's model, Boehm's model is divided in a hierarchy that at the top addresses the concerns of end-users and at the bottom is of interest to technically inclined personnel. The measurable properties and characteristics concentrate on highly technical details of quality while general utility is composed of as-is utility, maintainability, and portability [14] and tries to answer the questions:

- How well (easily, reliably, efficiently) can I use the software system as-is?
- How easy is it to maintain (understand, modify, and retest)?
- Can I still use it if I change my environment?

Although this model is a step forward, the characteristics *general utility* and *as-is utility* are far too generic and imprecise to be useful for defining verifiable requirements, which gives the model, similarly to McCall's, rather limited application in practical software quality engineering.

2.1.3.3 Dromey's Quality Model

Dromey's model [15] takes a different approach to software quality than the two previously presented models. For Dromey, a quality model should clearly be based upon the product perspective of quality:

> What must be recognized in any attempt to build a quality model is that software does not directly manifest quality attributes. Instead it exhibits product characteristic that imply or contribute to quality attributes and other characteristics (product defects) that detract from the quality attributes of a product. Most models of software quality fail to deal with the product characteristics side of the problem adequately and they also fail to make the direct links between quality attributes and corresponding product characteristics. [15]

Following this approach, Dromey has built a quality evaluation framework that analyzes the quality of software *components* through the measurement of tangible quality properties (Fig. 2.5). Each artifact produced in the software life cycle can be associated with a quality evaluation model. Dromey gives the following examples of what he means by software components for each of the different models:

- Variables, functions, statements, and so on can be considered components of the implementation model
- A requirement can be considered a component of the requirements model
- A module can be considered a component of the design model.

According to Dromey, these components all possess intrinsic properties that can be classified into four categories:

- Correctness: Evaluates if some basic principles are violated.
- Internal: Measures how well a component has been deployed according to its intended use.
- Contextual: Deals with the external influences by and on the use of a component.
- Descriptive: Measures the descriptiveness of a component (e.g., does it have a meaningful name?).

These properties are used to evaluate the quality of the components. This is illustrated in Fig. 2.6 for a variable component present in the implementation model.

It seems obvious from the inspection of the previous figures that Dromey's model is focused on the minute details of quality. This is stated explicitly:

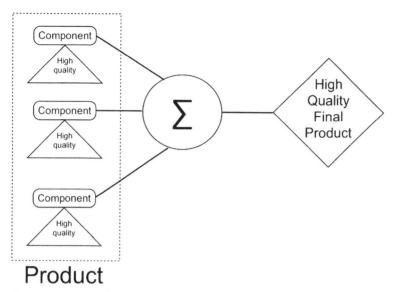

Product

Figure 2.5 Dromey's quality model (adapted from [15]).

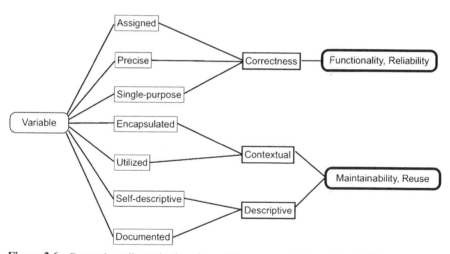

Figure 2.6 Dromey's quality evaluation of a variable component (adapted from [15]).

What we can do is identify and build in a consistent, harmonious, and complete set of product properties (such as modules without side effects) that result in manifestations of reliability and maintainability. [15]

For Dromey, the high-level characteristics of quality will manifest themselves if the components of the software product, from the individual requirements to the programming language variables, exhibit quality-carrying properties. This hypothesis can easily be contested. If all the components of all the artifacts produced during the software life cycle exhibit quality-carrying properties, will the resulting product manifest characteristics such as maintainability, functionality, and others?

The following analogy will be useful in answering this question: If you buy the highest quality flour, along with the highest quality apples and the highest quality cinnamon, will you automatically produce an apple pie that is of the highest quality?

The answer is obviously negative. In addition to quality ingredients, at least three more elements are needed in order to produce an apple pie of high quality:

- A recipe (i.e., an overall architecture and an execution process). Dromey acknowledges this by identifying process maturity as a desirable high-level characteristic. However, it is rather briefly mentioned in his publications on the subject.

- The consumer's tastes must be taken into account. In order for the result to be considered of high quality by the consumer, it needs to be tuned to his or her tastes. This is akin to what is commonly called user needs in software engineering. User needs are completely ignored by Dromey.

- Someone with the qualifications and the tools to properly execute the recipe.

Although Dromey's work is interesting from a technically inclined stakeholder's perspective, it is difficult to see how it could be used at the beginning of the lifecycle to determine user quality needs. In Reference 15, Dromey states that software quality "must be considered in a systematic and structured way, from the tangible to the intangible." By focusing too much on the tangible, Dromey overlooked the aspects allowing one to build a model that is meaningful for stakeholders typically involved at the beginning of the lifecycle. Therefore, this model is rather unwieldy to specify user quality needs and it fails to qualify as useful for software quality engineering according to the established requirements. This does not mean that it cannot be useful later on as a checklist for ensuring that product quality is up to standards. It can definitely be classified as a bottom-to-top approach to software quality.

2.1.3.4   ISO/IEC 9126 Quality Model

In 1991, the International Organization for Standardization (ISO) introduced a standard named ISO/IEC 9126 (1991): Software product evaluation – Quality characteristics and guidelines for their use. This standard aimed to define a quality model for software and a set of guidelines for measuring the characteristics associated with it. ISO/IEC 9126 quickly gained IT specialists' interest; however, some important problems were associated with its first release:

- There were no guidelines on how to provide an overall assessment of quality
- There were no indications on how to perform measurements of the quality characteristics
- The model reflected mostly a developer's view of software.

In order to address these concerns, ISO/IEC JTC1 committee SC7 began working on a revision of the standard, creating in time its new, four-part version:

- ISO/IEC 9126-1: defines an updated quality model [7].
- ISO/IEC 9126-2: defines a set of external measures [16].
- ISO/IEC 9126-3: defines a set of internal measures [17].
- ISO/IEC 9126-4: defines a set of quality in use measures [18].

The new quality model defined in ISO/IEC 9126-1 recognizes three aspects of software quality and defines them as follows:

- Quality in use:

  Quality in use is the user's view of the quality of the software product when it is used in a specific environment and a specific context of use. It measures the extent to which users can achieve their goals in a particular environment, rather than measuring the properties of the software itself. [18]

- External quality:

  External quality is the totality of characteristics of the software product from an external view. It is the quality when the software is executed, which is typically measured and evaluated while testing in a simulated environment with simulated data using external metrics. [16]

- Internal quality:

  Internal quality is the totality of attributes of a product that determine its ability to satisfy stated and implied needs when used under specified conditions. Details of software product quality can be improved during code implementation, reviewing and testing, but the fundamental nature of the software product quality represented by the internal quality remains unchanged unless redesigned. [17]

The ISO/IEC 9126 internal and external quality model (Fig. 2.7) is a three-layer model composed of quality characteristics, quality subcharacteristics, and quality

Figure 2.7   ISO/IEC 9126 internal and external quality model (adapted from [7]).

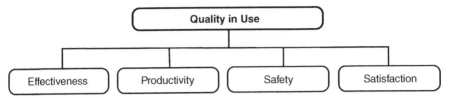

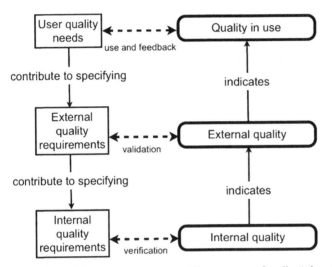

Figure 2.8   ISO/IEC 9126 quality in use model (adapted from [7]).

Figure 2.9   Relationships between the different aspects of quality (adapted from [7]).

measures. More than 200 measures of internal and external quality were proposed as part of the standard. It is important to note that the measures do not make an exhaustive set, which means that other measures can also be used.

The part of the model dedicated to an end user, called further quality in use (Fig. 2.8), is a two-layer model composed of characteristics and quality measures. Theoretically, internal quality, external quality and quality in use are linked together in a predictive model shown in Fig. 2.9.

This prediction relationship states that once the requirements are established and software construction is underway, the quality model can be used to predict the overall quality. In reality, no model may claim to follow perfectly this prediction mechanism. In case of ISO/IEC 9126, the links between internal and external quality seem rather obvious, as they share the same model, however the links between external quality and quality in use are more of a cause–effect nature and as such are much more difficult to predict, especially when the prediction begins on the internal quality level.

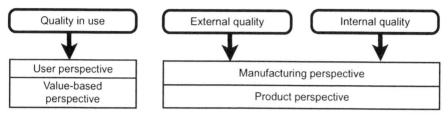

Figure 2.10 Relationships between ISO/IEC 9126 and the perspectives of quality.

It is interesting to see how the three aspects of quality defined in ISO/IEC 9126 relate to five perspectives of quality defined by Kitchenham and Pfleeger:

- ISO/IEC 9126-4, which defines quality in use, is directly related to the user and value-based perspectives. The definition of the user perspective of quality states that it is concerned with the appropriateness of a product for a given context of use. Quality in use is defined as the capability of the software product to enable specified users to achieve specified goals in specified contexts of use. The relationship between the two is clear. Quality in use and the value-based perspective of quality are linked essentially through the *satisfaction* characteristic. This characteristic inherently recognizes that quality can have a different meaning and/or value for different stakeholders. Satisfaction levels can thus be set according to those levels of perception.

- ISO/IEC 9126-3, which defines internal quality, and ISO/IEC 9126-2, which defines external quality, are directly related to both the manufacturing and product perspectives. The definitions of the quality characteristics *functionality* and *reliability* can be linked with the manufacturing perspective of quality. Reliability, usability, efficiency, maintainability, and portability are all inherent characteristics of the product and a manifestation of the product perspective of quality.

The presented analysis of the ISO/IEC 9126 model shows (Fig. 2.10) that four out of the five Kitchenham/Pfleeger perspectives of quality are addressed, but does ISO/IEC 9126 address the transcendental perspective of quality? At this point, the following statement could be in order: As the transcendental perspective of quality cannot be defined, it cannot be explicitly implemented in a software product. However, the transcendental aspect of quality will emerge when a holistic approach to quality engineering is taken.

So, is the quality model of ISO/IEC 9126 useful for software quality engineering? The simple conclusion is *yes*. Besides being useful for software quality engineering, the ISO/IEC 9126 model brings several important practical benefits:

- It is a "consensus" model. It was developed by specialists from the international community of software engineering and as such has international recognition.

- It takes an incremental approach to software quality that begins with quality in use, something that is easy to grasp for nontechnical stakeholders, and ends with internal quality, something with which more technically inclined stakeholders will feel more comfortable.

- It offers a comprehensive set of suggested measures that allow for the assessment of software quality.

The model in its latest version together with all accompanying standards has now been publicly available for almost a decade, which, in the life of software quality, is a very long period without substantial modifications. Taking this into consideration, ISO/IEC JTC1 SC7 undertook in the early 2000s an effort to modernize its whole set of quality-related standards. As the result the development of a new series of standards, ISO/IEC 25000 SQuaRE—System and software quality requirements and evaluation [19], was initiated in 2001, with the chief document among them being ISO/IEC 25010—Systems and Software Quality Models [26].

2.1.3.5 ISO/IEC 25010 SQuaRE Systems and Software Quality Models

ISO/IEC 25010 [20] continues the approach used in the development of ISO/IEC 9126 and similarly to it proposes two distinct perspectives, each of which has its own model. The first perspective is related to the use of the software or system with the model called *quality in use* model, the second is related to the system or software itself and has its *system/software product quality* model.

The quality in use model is composed of five characteristics (see Fig. 2.11) and eleven measures. The objective of this model is to define characteristics that relate to the outcome of interaction between the user and the system in a given context of use. In simpler terms, quality in use model refers to *business use* of the system, the context that is intended as information technology-free. This model is applicable to the complete human-computer system, including both computer systems in use and software products in use. The comparison of ISO/IEC 9126 and ISO/IEC 25010 quality in use models shows that the newest edition has not only one characteristic more but also several new related measures.

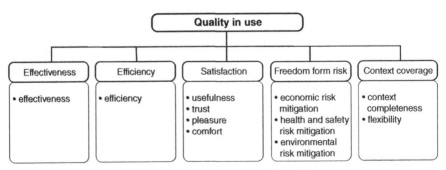

Figure 2.11   ISO/IEC 25010 quality in use model (adapted from [20]).

The product quality model is composed of eight characteristics, which are further subdivided into subcharacteristics that relate to static properties of software and dynamic properties of the system or software, if that is the case (Fig. 2.12).

In comparison with ISO/IEC 9126 internal and external quality model, the ISO/IEC 25010 product quality model uses different terminology that, however, keeps a similar meaning:

- *Static* corresponds to *internal* and applies to the software under development (not being executed or run)
- *Dynamic* corresponds to *external* and applies to a system or software being actually executed, but not within the operation context (for this there is the quality-in-use model).

Due to this similarity, further in this book both terminologies will be used alternately.

As can be easily found, the ISO/IEC 25010 product quality model not only has more characteristics than its predecessor but also some subcharacteristics were added or modified.

The standard indicates several important practical-application features:

- "the characteristics defined by both models are relevant to all software products and computer systems"
- "characteristics and subcharacteristics provide consistent terminology for specifying, measuring and evaluating system and software product quality"
- "they also provide a set of quality characteristics against which stated quality requirements can be compared for completeness."

The intended application of both presented quality models is principally the support for specification of quality requirements and evaluation of software and software-intensive computer systems from different perspectives, such as those of the developers, acquirers, or independent evaluators. From a development perspective, using quality models brings several tangible benefits, among them help in identifying software and system requirements, validating the comprehensiveness of a requirements definition, identifying software and system design objectives, identifying software and system testing objectives, or identifying acceptance criteria for a software product and/or software-intensive computer system. From a software quality engineering perspective, three benefits are crucial:

- Definition of quality requirements
- Identification of measures of quality characteristics in support of these requirements
- Establishment of acceptance criteria.

As the ISO/IEC 9126 quality model has earlier been classified as useful for software quality engineering, its modernized version, ISO/IEC 25010, is also recognized as such.

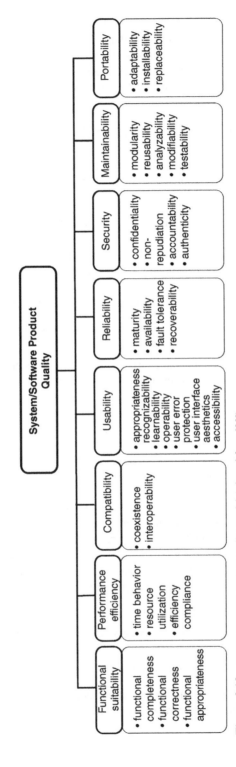

Figure 2.12 ISO/IEC 25010 product quality model (adapted from [20]).

2.1.4 Quality Measurement

Measurement requires both particular knowledge and commitment. As measurement activities are too often considered in software engineering to be nonproductive, or worse, disturbing the already nervous rhythm of development, to execute the measurement an organization must take a "conscious" decision to dedicate and assign resources, budget, and time to it. One of the most well-known measurement processes addressing these concerns (organizational view) has been developed and proposed by ISO/IEC JTC1 Subcommittee 7 (SC7)—System and Software Engineering. The model published in the international standard ISO/IEC 15939 is shown in Fig. 2.13 [21].

As can be noticed, the first and foremost activity required when intending to execute measurement on the organization level is the *commitment*. The very fundamental question, however, is: Why measure? What are the benefits of measuring in software engineering? The most-known outcomes are:

- Effective and precise communication
- Means to control and supervise projects
- Quick identification of problems and their eventual resolutions
- Taking complex decisions based on data, not on guesses
- Rational justification of decisions.

Although this approach is principally of an organizational nature, it requires in its executive part ("plan and perform measurement process") particular, technical knowledge. The measurement process, to render valid and usable results, should be executed in a professional and scientifically sound manner. Again, ISO/IEC JTC1

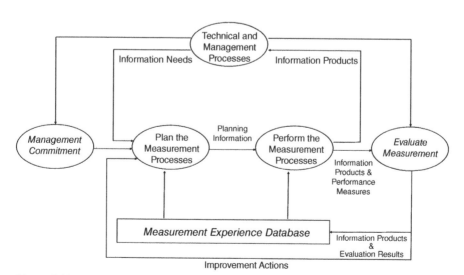

Figure 2.13   Software measurement process model (adapted from [21]).

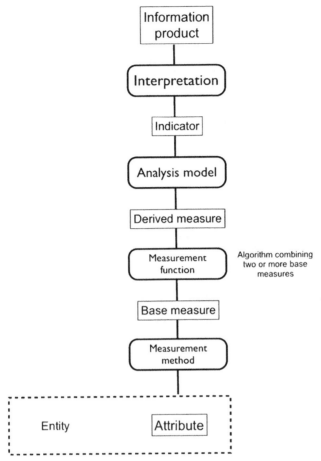

Figure 2.14   Generic measurement model from ISO/IEC 15939 (adapted from [21]).

SC7 has proposed a generic measurement model (Fig. 2.14) that gained international acceptance and quickly became the best practice in the domain of software measurement. The model helps to transit from the point of identification of measurable attributes, through measurement methods and analysis activities, to finally reach the phase of *information product*. This last result is the most important outcome of the whole process, as it is used to take a decision.

In software quality engineering, measurement is a pivotal concept. In other words, quality cannot be effectively engineered without measurement as measurement makes the only objective means to verify the presence of quality in a developed software product.

This rather obvious statement gained its formal representation in both academic and industrial research, resulting in development and publication of three measurement-dedicated parts of one of the most well-known international standards dedicated to software quality: ISO/IEC 9126. For the same reasons for which the

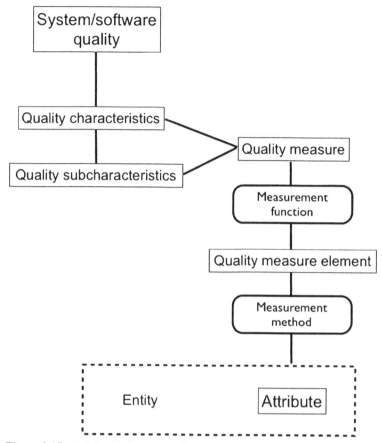

Figure 2.15 Relationship between quality measures and quality model from ISO/IEC 9126 and ISO/IEC 25010 (adapted from [22]).

quality model from ISO/IEC 9126 was modified and replaced by the one from ISO/IEC 25010, the measures published in ISO/IEC 9126-2, -3, and -4 are being actually revised and updated to reflect the rapid evolution in information technologies. The new standards from the ISO/IEC 25000 SQuaRE series proposing the measures for quality in use (ISO/IEC 25022) and product quality (ISO/IEC 25023) are expected to be publicly available in 2014.

Both measures (called in ISO/IEC 9126 "metrics") and measurement processes presented in the standard adhere closely to the generic measurement process published in ISO/IEC 15939, which guarantees their professional soundness. Figure 2.15 illustrates how quality measures being taken following this generic process relate to the structure of the quality model published in ISO/IEC 9126-1 and ISO/IEC 25010.

The most important issue arises, however, when a software quality engineer attempts to really measure the quality. His or her primary concerns usually are:

Figure 2.16 Software product quality life cycle and related measures (adapted from [22]).

- What to measure
- How to measure
- Where to seek support (practical or scientific).

One of ways to address these concerns would be to use as a practical, widely "digested" support what is offered in ISO/IEC 9126. The standard proposes three distinctive perspectives of analyzing the quality of a software product (internal quality, external quality, and quality in use) discussed in earlier chapters of this book, associates with each of these perspectives a large amount of measures to choose from, and gives some recommendations about how to interpret obtained results. It also, as is shown in Fig. 2.16, positions quality perspectives and their measures against each other both in requirement definition and implementation phases.

This statement may create a false impression that ISO/IEC 9126 is *the* solution to all pains a software quality engineer may suffer. It is then very important to repeat that ISO/IEC 9126 is being in fact replaced (as of the date of publication of this book) by a new series of software quality specialized standards called ISO/IEC 25000 SQuaRE—Software Product Quality Requirements and Evaluation, which offers to the user not only the quality model and associated measures but also enhanced support in guidance, measurement practice, evaluation, and management.

2.1.5 Quality Evaluation

The evaluation of software product quality is important to both the acquisition and development of software. The essential parts of the software quality evaluation process are:

- The quality model
- The method of evaluation
- Software measurement
- Supporting tools.

For anyone attempting to execute a software quality evaluation, it is important to remember that an evaluation never goes alone. It must be coupled with measurement designed and tailored precisely to purposes of the evaluation. It is also important to realize that an evaluation is a complex task that should follow a well-defined process and plan. A model for such a process (Fig. 2.17) has been developed by ISO/IEC JTC1 SC7 and published in ISO/IEC 25040 [23] as the part of ISO/IEC 25000 SQuaRE series of standards and as the modernization of the model published in ISO/IEC 14598-1 Information Technology—Software Product

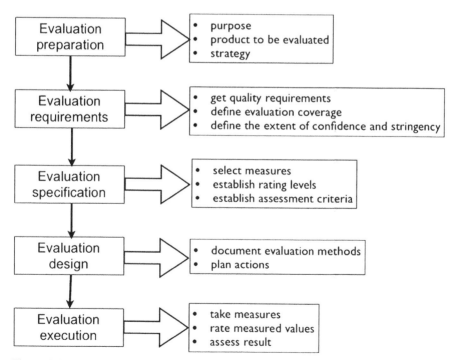

Figure 2.17 ISO/IEC 25040 SQuaRE model for generic software quality evaluation process (adapted from [23]).

Evaluation—General Overview [24]. Even if in the industrial practice the evaluation can be conducted from different perspectives (such as that of a developer, acquirer, or independent evaluator), all of them follow this model, as it represents the generic approach to quality evaluation.

The ultimate purpose of any evaluation it to obtain reliable information allowing for making a wise and justified decision in actual situation. In software quality the "actual situation" often refers to the type of intermediate or final software product to be evaluated, which in turn points to the stage in the life cycle and the purpose of the evaluation. For a software product in its context of use, quality in use should be evaluated, for a software product as a part of a system in operation external (or *dynamic)* quality should be evaluated and, finally, static artifacts of a software product in development would require an evaluation of internal (or *static)* quality.

A professionally conducted evaluation would require a good plan in order to achieve its goals within predefined time and budget. Some elements, such as the following, should be taken into consideration when building such a plan:

- Participants involved in the evaluation
- Budget
- Expected evaluation outcome (or information products)
- Schedule and milestones
- Responsibilities of participants
- Evaluation methods, tools, and standards
- Management of the evaluation project.

Within the evaluation process itself, the first and rather important activity is establishing evaluation requirements with the objective of defining software product quality requirements that are the subject of the quality evaluation. This definition should additionally take into account such criteria as evaluation budget, target date for the evaluation, purpose of the evaluation, and criticality of the software product.

Evaluation requirements are further translated into a specification of an evaluation. The purpose of the evaluation specification is to define the set of measures to be applied to the software product and its components during measurement activities as well as assessment criteria. This includes:

- Selecting measures
- Establishing rating levels for measures
- Establishing criteria for assessment.

In other words, a specification indicates what and how to measure, the targeted (or reference) values for measures, and how to interpret (assess) the results.

Before the actual execution, similarly to what happens in a development process, the evaluation has to be designed. The purpose of such a design is principally to adjust the evaluation plan through considering the measurement to be applied. This is achieved through:

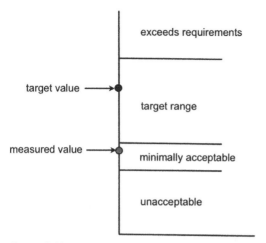

Figure 2.18   Example of an evaluation scale (adapted from [53]).

- Documenting evaluation methods
- Rescheduling evaluation actions.

In this moment an evaluation is fully prepared and the execution may begin. The objective of this phase is to obtain evaluation results from measuring the software product as defined in the evaluation specification and as planned in the evaluation plan. The selected measures are applied to the software product and components, resulting in values on the measurement scales. The measured values are mapped into the rating level scale as established (see an example in Fig. 2.18). Assessment is then applied, where rated levels are summarized in the form of performance levels of quality characteristics being the subject of the evaluation. The result is a statement of the extent to which the software product meets quality requirements.

Further, in a decisional process the summarized quality may be complemented by other aspects such as time and cost. Finally, a managerial decision is made based on the managerial criteria. The result of a managerial decision may be the acceptance or rejection of a software product, modification of release plan, or even withdrawing from the production.

2.2 ENGINEERING OF SOFTWARE QUALITY

The quality of a software product or system does not come automatically as a result of the development process. Quite often to the contrary, the development process is a culprit for continuous deterioration of final quality of software. Especially the processes that possess "quick fix" actions tend to dramatically diminish quality of their outcome, as they neither pay enough attention to identifying quality requirements nor take enough time to make the quality happen. It is then rather important to understand that obtaining quality in a software product or system is an engineering effort, quite similar in its form and objectives to developing a product or system and as such should have adequate ramifications, resources, processes, models, and practices.

To help the presentation of subjects discussed in following chapters, a simplified pattern of practical steps to follow based on software life cycle phases proposed in ISO/IEC 15288:2008 [25] is introduced in the following.

Discovery Phase. In this phase, the basic two sets of requirements should be identified and defined:

- Functional and nonfunctional requirements of the product
- Quality in use requirements.

It is important to note here that according to the model of software quality life cycle defined in both ISO/IEC 9126-1 and ISO/IEC 25010 (Fig. 2.16), the requirements of quality in use contribute to specifying external (dynamic) quality requirements, which in turn contribute to specifying internal (static) quality requirements. This indicates that the attributes of quality in use have a direct impact on the technical and technological decisions that will have to be made when the development process starts. This requires that quality in use characteristics be analyzed, applicable measures identified, and target values for each of them assigned. The ISO standard that can be applied to complete this task is ISO/IEC 9126-4 quality in use metrics [18] or ISO/IEC 25022 [26], when published.

Quality in use requirements help define success criteria of a new software product only if their final set and respective targeted values are the major milestone and contributor in the definition of functional and nonfunctional requirements of the future software product with the *user perception of the software product quality* already "sewn" into the overall definition.

Requirements Analysis Phase. In this phase, the applicable quality requirements define external (dynamic) and internal (static) quality attributes of the software product to be developed. The ISO standards supporting this phase are ISO/IEC 9126-2 external quality metrics [16], ISO/IEC 9126-3 internal quality metrics [17], or ISO/IEC 25023 [27], when published.

It has to be stressed here that, as will be further discussed in Section 2.2.1, the attributes of both external and internal quality identified in this phase are only direct descendants of quality in use requirements, and as such are not a complete list of all quality requirements necessary for a given software or system. A simple illustration of this limitation would be the following question: What is the chance of identifying a particular static (internal) quality requirement applied, for example, to the level of code complexity when talking to the customer about his or her business needs? Obviously slim to none, but this requirement may eventually need to be defined, and the place for it is further in the project life cycle.

Architectural Design Phase. In this phase, the requirements identified in previous phases undergo a scrutiny from two different perspectives: feasibility and completeness. The feasibility analysis has the objective of sifting wishful thinking from hard reality. Not every quality in use requirement can be translated into obtainable external (dynamic) quality attribute(s), be it due to technological constraints or budgetary ones. On the other hand, the analysis of dynamic (external) quality requirements obtained in the way of decomposing quality in use requirements, when they are confronted with the functional architectural design, may prove them incomplete. So the discussion between the software quality engineer and the architect may help identify the requirements that could not have been seen on the level of negotiations with the user. This part of the architectural design phase helps finalize the list of dynamic quality requirements. What happens to static quality requirements? As they share the quality model with dynamic quality requirements, they can be much more easily further identified and detailed, but the list still would not be complete. To finalize the list, the program design part of the architectural design phase has to be taken into consideration. On this level the static (internal) quality requirements obtained through decomposition of dynamic quality requirements should be exposed to exactly the same scrutiny of feasibility and completeness, however this time in discussions with the developers.

The final set of requirements has to be transformed now into a set of engineering "to dos" that can be communicated to the engineering staff (architects, testers, developers).

This phase has a rather limited support from published ISO standards, however, quality models and quality measures come in handy, especially as tools helping scrutinize quality requirements.

Implementation Phase. This phase as the first in the whole life cycle creates *a product* that can be measured and evaluated. The created product is intermediate and changes many times before becoming a ready-to-use solution, but exactly due to this fact it is critical to measure and evaluate its quality. Every iteration with measured and evaluated quality produces indications yielding further improvements. Measurement of internal (static) quality (and, if needed, external quality) attributes defined in the requirements analysis phase are supported by the ISO/IEC 9126-2 and -3 [16, 17] and ISO/IEC 25023 [27], when published.

The process of measurement and evaluation of the quality of the developed software (or system) is supported, depending on the position of the evaluating entity, by ISO/IEC 14598-3 process for developers [28], 14598-4 process for acquirers [29], 14598-5 process for evaluators [30], ISO/IEC 25040 Evaluation process [23], and ISO/IEC 25041 Evaluation guide for developers, acquirers, and independent evaluators [31]. Whenever it is possible, the use of the last two documents is recommended.

The measurement and evaluation are also supported by the documentation modules published in ISO/IEC 14598-6 [32] and ISO/IEC 25042 Evaluation modules [33], when published.

The results of measurements of chosen quality attributes are compared with target values assigned to them in previous phases and the conclusions are presented to development teams as the corrective measures of improvement.

The objective of the **Integration Phase** is to link all components of the software or system and verify that they are able to correctly communicate. It is useful to keep in mind that the final result of the integration phase is not the system or software yet, it is still the collection of components that simply know how to talk to each other. From the perspective of quality engineering the possible interventions should be analyzed through the process of integration tests. The tests usually find two categories of reasons for wrong behavior of structures of modules being linked: internal, related to module architecture or coding, and external, more related to higher level architecture that puts the modules together. If the terms "external" and "internal" are replaced respectively by "dynamic" and "static," the areas of possible quality engineering interventions appear obvious. The integration phase marks the only moment at which static and dynamic quality may be measured and verified at the same time, but due to the nature of the phase itself only a few attributes can be taken in account. Similarly to the architectural design phase, this phase has rather limited support from published ISO standards, but of course quality models and quality measures are in recommended use.

Verification Phase. The product is integrated and stakeholder's functional, nonfunctional, and external (dynamic) quality requirements have to be satisfied in this phase. The process of the evaluation requires a similar procedure as internal (static) quality evaluation in the previous phase and is being similarly well supported by standardization instruments (ISO/IEC 9126-2 [16] or ISO/IEC 25023 [27], when published).

The results of measurements of external quality attributes are compared with target values assigned to them in previous phases and the resulting conclusions are presented as the corrective measures of improvement. The feedback may be directed to different phases of the process depending on the level of the severity of discrepancies between required and obtained external quality.

The **Validation Phase** moves the software product to the business level, where the user validates its usefulness for conducting his business, usually with no regard to technicalities. This means that quality in use requirements have to be satisfied "here and now." The process of the evaluation of quality in use requires the same procedure as external quality evaluation and is being equally well supported by standardization instruments. The only difference is in using ISO/IEC 9126 – Part 4 [18] instead of ISO/IEC 9126 – Part 2, or ISO/IEC 25022 instead of ISO/IEC 25023, when published.

The results of measurements of quality in use attributes are compared with target values assigned to them in previous phases. The resulting conclusions may be used as the corrective measures of improvement. The feedback may be directed to different phases of the process depending on the level of the severity of discrepancies between required and obtained quality in use.

The **Transition Phase** has the purpose "to establish a capability to provide services specified by stakeholder requirements in the operational environment" [25]. The processes of this phase end when a fully operational instance of the software or product is installed in the production environment of the user. The possible interventions of quality engineering are rather scarce, principally limited to particular quality attributes, such as *installability* or *portability*.

The **Operation and Maintenance Phase** is the longest phase of the life of a system or software. During this phase the system is exposed to the harshest tests, which are not only long and continuous but also much more "creative" than the ones designed by the tester of the developing organization. In practice anything and everything may happen when a group of normal, IT-uninterested users begin to execute their duties (and their habits) so, in fact, every category of software quality engineering intervention may be called to action in one moment or the other, depending on the type of the event.

For example, the real change in the user's productivity (quality in use) when using the system will manifest itself after some time, the resource utilization (dynamic quality) may prove inefficient under the stress of too many real (not simulated) concurrent users, the maintainability of the code (static quality) may show inadequate when too many interventions (to comply with user critics or requirements) need to be applied.

Measurement and evaluation of quality in the operation and maintenance phase make sense, especially if we take into consideration that validation and verification phases where quality is being measured and evaluated for the first time happen in relatively short periods of time with limited exploration opportunities (e.g., a limited number of users), however, the important question in this case would be "how long?"

The structure "product-user" usually reaches its level of stability after few months of exploitation so it makes sense to conduct relatively frequent quality measurements and evaluations through a similar period. Further, equally frequent measurement efforts probably would not deliver substantial data due to the "routinization" of interaction between the user and the product, but a professional approach to the maintenance of the system requires at least monitoring (periodic verification) of quality in use and dynamic quality. The measurement and evaluation procedure for quality in the operation and maintenance phase would be the same as proposed for all other phases. The evaluation results can be useful both immediately (*evolutional* role of maintenance process) and in a long-term perspective, when a new product or its release will be considered.

Some concise advice on how to apply software quality engineering along the phases of the generic system life cycle is proposed in the Consolidated Quality Life Cycle (CQL) model, discussed more in detail in Section 2.3.5.

2.2.1 Software Quality Requirements

The first and often most difficult point of software quality engineering projects is the identification of quality requirements. It has already been stated in this book that the user (or, more widely, the stakeholder) is rarely, if ever, in a position to discuss all these "-ities" with which the subject of quality is infested. If we asked an average, IT-illiterate software system user what would be his or her requirements for quality, it is very probable that the answers would be, "I want quality to be high" or "No blue screens, no freezing, absolutely no lost or corrupted data." A "no blue screens" answer is in fact not entirely bad, as a good quality engineer would link it quickly to one of the "-ities," namely to *reliability*, but an "I want quality to be high" answer is hopeless and requires serious digging in order to identify the quality components, or aspects that would altogether constitute "high quality" as seen by our interlocutor. In the majority of real cases, *digging* is what happens during the process of software quality requirement definition.

2.2.1.1   What Are Quality Requirements?

Before discussing software quality requirements, it is important to define requirement as opposed to need. As M. Azuma stated (personal communication):

> Needs for a product are expectations of stakeholders for the effects of the product when it is actually operated, which means such actions to the software product as development, distribution, release, installation, use and maintenance.

Going further, needs may be divided into stated needs and implied needs and both should be transformed into requirements. The difference between needs and requirements may be illustrated by the following definition: "Requirements are the external specification of specific needs that a product is expected to satisfy."

Figure 2.19 illustrates relationship between needs and requirements. Stakeholders' needs (stated and implied) are collected and identified, then transformed in functional and quality requirements.

In *Guide to SWEBOK* [34], "software quality" refers to user requirements or levels of fitness for use or customer satisfaction. In all these definitions, the same key point is considered: requirements and stakeholder needs. Furthermore, when defining software quality fundamentals, the guide points out the ability of the

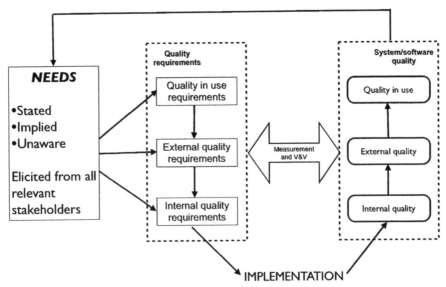

Figure 2.19   Relationship between needs and quality requirements (adapted from [34]).

software engineer to understand quality concepts when developing or maintaining software. It also denotes the prime importance of customer's requirements, which include quality requirements: "the software engineer has a responsibility to elicit quality requirements which may not be explicit at the outset and to discuss their importance as well as the level of difficulty in attaining them."

On the other hand, the guide defines nonfunctional software requirements as "the ones that act to constrain the solution, also sometimes known as constraints or quality requirements."

Emergence of software quality requirements as a separate category began somewhere in the last decade when requirement engineering encountered difficulties in capturing all of the types (such as functional, performance, organizational, or quality). First, the difficulty was associated with the nonfunctional requirements and supplementary requirements, which where attached to functional requirements. Later, nonfunctional requirements were associated with quality requirements, where more research concentrated on their modeling and representation and on negotiation of conflicts between different categories of requirements.

As the result, as is indicated in Reference 35, "identifying quality requirements that can be elicited, formalized and further evaluated in each phase of full software product lifecycle became a crucial task in the process of building a high quality software product."

2.2.1.2   Elicitation, Identification, and Definition of Quality Requirements

Quality requirements may possess distinctive features that differentiate them from other categories of requirements, but there is one important tool that all of them usually share: the identification/formalization process. This process tool [36], as shown in the example in Fig. 2.20, identifies all phases or actions necessary to

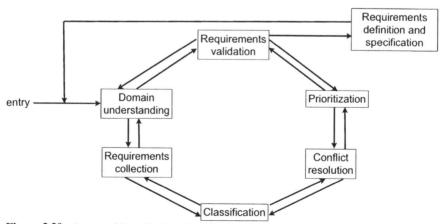

Figure 2.20   Process of formalization of requirements (adapted from [36]).

produce a valid and reliable list or requirements, despite their nature. If properly followed, the process produces a full dossier associated with requirements, beginning with solid knowledge of the application domain (understanding the application sector helps in identifying requirements), through collection, classification, and prioritization of requirements ending by an agreed and accepted list of valid and feasible requirements.

Before, however, the interception and identification of quality requirements occur it is necessary to know the perspectives (or categories) of quality in which these requirements will be sought and placed, when found. What immediately comes to mind is the application of a quality model, treated in this situation as a "menu" helping to set up the research area. There is, of course, a freedom of choice from different existing models; however, the practical decision must take into account the existence of verification mechanisms associated with the model of choice, the existence of measures that will allow for verification of the realization of identified quality requirements. From this perspective the earlier discussed models from ISO/IEC 9126 and ISO/IEC 25010 seem to be some of the better choices, and as such, they will be further used in this chapter.

It is perhaps worthwhile to position quality requirements (based on our choice of quality model) within the overall structure of software requirements. In most cases the requirements definition phase begins with discussions at a high level of abstraction, sometimes called "business vision," where stakeholders express their requirements in business, service, and quite often usability-related terms. It is then the responsibility of an analyst to "translate" such nontechnical information into a technical representation useful in development project. As presented in Fig. 2.21, this translation may produce three immediate categories of requirements: functional, nonfunctional (quality excluded), and quality requirements. It is to be stressed that

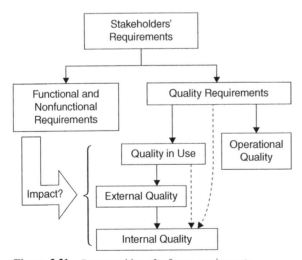

Figure 2.21 Decomposition of software requirements.

the traditional categorization of quality requirements (usually only few, arbitrarily chosen) as "nonfunctional" is replaced here by a separate, distinctive category of quality requirements. The latter may be further broken down, according to ISO/IEC 9126 and ISO/IEC 25010, into quality in use, external (dynamic), and internal (static) quality requirements. In case of massive deployment of a software product it may be worthwhile to consider the fourth category of quality requirements— operational quality requirements. This category, based on definitions published by QuEST Forum in TL 9000 standards [37], identifies quality attributes associated with statistical parameters of software usage. TL 9000—Quality Management System Measurement Handbook proposes four categories of requirements and/or measurements applicable to software products:

- Common measurements: referring to number of problems reported, response time, overdue problem responsiveness, and on-time delivery
- Hardware and software measurements: referring to system outage
- Software measurements: referring to software installation and maintenance
- Service measurement: referring to service quality.

Again, a software engineer is absolutely free to choose his or her quality requirements decomposition schema, but if this decision is not supported by measures, the choice is void.

One of the important questions a software engineer may ask when beginning a development project could be: Why should quality requirements be treated separately and what makes them different from all other types of requirements? The simple answer is: Although (ideally speaking) functional and nonfunctional requirements could be complete and "frozen" before actually any development starts (Fig. 2.22), the quality requirements are, in fact, partial.

Let us examine what categories of quality requirements can be identified when discussing with a stakeholder his "business vision":

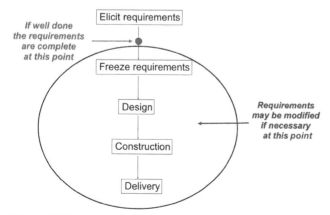

Figure 2.22   Ideal execution of functional requirement definition.

- Operational quality requirements. If the software product to be developed is planned for a large population of users, this category is valid and the analyst may seek more details to identify related requirements. If developed software is personalized, singular, or will be deployed in small quantity, this category is void, as no statistically valid data will be available.

- Quality-in-use requirements. As this category represents purely application context-oriented quality requirements, the "business vision" is a good and usually rich source of information. Most quality-in-use requirements could and should be identified in this phase.

- External (dynamic) quality requirements. This perspective of quality refers to a software product that is complete and operational, but observed from a technical perspective (like that of a technical support or maintenance team). As the software product does not physically exist yet and a business vision-oriented stakeholder is usually not able to give enough information to immediately identify external quality requirements, these requirements must be sought either through "deduction" from quality in use requirements (results are always partial) or further in the development cycle, when more technical information is available (such as high- and mid-level architectural design). There is, however, one very interesting exception: usability. This quality characteristic is classified in ISO/IEC 9126 as "external" (or *dynamic* in ISO/IEC 24010) but in several facets it represents end user concerns and can be clearly expressed by a stakeholder in the phase of "business vision." For example, as stated originally in the standard, "an external learnability [metric] should be able to assess how long users take to learn how to use particular functions, and the effectiveness of help systems and documentation," which can be expressed very early in the requirements definition phase.

- Internal (static) quality requirements. This perspective of quality applies to static artifacts such as code, low-level design, and documentation, and there is little chance to gather any useful information from a business vision-oriented stakeholder. To identify external quality requirements, these requirements must be sought either through "deduction" from external quality requirements (results are often relatively rich) or further in the development cycle, when more technical information is available (e.g., detailed program design).

This analysis (presented in Fig. 2.23), by illustrating a rather specific nature of quality requirements signals that software quality engineering processes, may considerably differ from those associated with classical software development.

2.2.1.3 *From a Requirement to a Measure*

When asking a software engineer from the industry the most difficult part of the effort to "engineer" quality into a software product, one may receive responses like these (quoted from the author's experience):

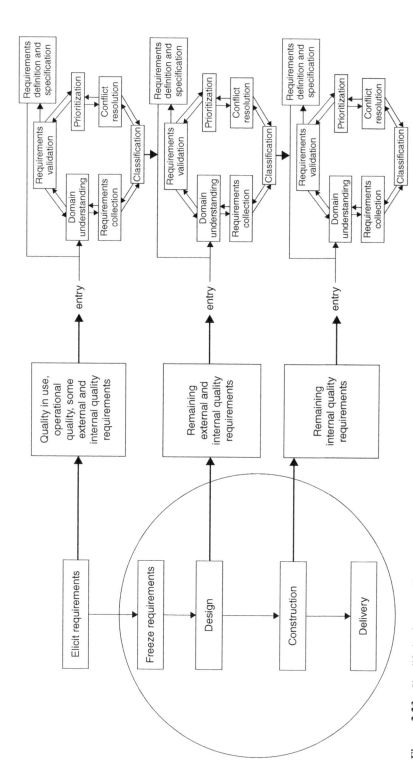

Figure 2.23 Simplified software quality requirements identification/definition process.

- Identification and further definition of quality requirements
- Translating requirements into something tangible and verifiable (let us call it "measures")
- Making it happen, which translates into methods, processes, and sometimes even banal recipes of developing software systems that actually *have* quality in them
- Verifying that required quality is in fact there (let us call it "evaluation").

The fact that the definition of quality requirements is on this list of answers raises another question: Is it really so difficult to "squeeze" from a business story the information required to at least start defining quality requirements?

To answer this question we will use the results of an experiment repeated continuously for last eight years, in which software engineering masters students participating in the software quality engineering course at École de technologie supérieure (Montreal, Canada) are asked to identify within a 30-minute period as many quality requirements as possible from a simple business vision story presented by a windows manufacturer. To make the story even more realistic, the manufacturer is absolute ignorant in anything even loosely related to IT.

The windows manufacturer presented his business vision by indicating services that are required from his new IT system:

A. Control manufacturing process 24/7

B. Allow for ERP-type production supervision

C. Control and manage export of ready products, including adding new offices in other countries

D. Offer an online ordering service

E. Offer an online follow-up service for active orders.

The results obtained during the experiment were very similar in all eight sessions:

- When identifying applicable quality categories, the students with no exception ruled out the operational and internal quality, focusing on quality in use and external quality
- In the first 15 minutes of the experiment, most of them identified the requirement of reliability (service A), security (services D and E), and portability (service C)
- In the next 10 minutes they added learnability, understandability, and maintainability (referring to customer's IT ignorance and international expansion ambitions)
- In the last 5 minutes they additionally identified productivity (service B), recoverability (all services), and adaptability (service C).

As amazing as these results may be, they are neither exhaustive nor complete but still they carry an interesting indicator: they suggest that the real problem in software quality requirements identification and definition may not entirely be due to the unquestionable complexity of the subject. It may partially lay in missing "quality engineering awareness," still so typical to the contemporary IT industry. This complicated sentence may also be rephrased in less formal and friendlier way: It is not so complicated; just give it a chance and try!

Well, if they tried and succeeded, there still is some work to do before a software product exhibits real quality: the identification of quality attributes and corresponding measures that should be applied and later measured in course of the development project.

It has to be stated clearly that there is no recipe for choosing the measures, but the challenge is smaller while requirements are known. It resembles in some sense deciding what one will eat when going to a restaurant. If the requirements were "cold seafood" the client would not go to "Texas Steakhouse" but rather to a Japanese restaurant and seek sushi.

2.2.1.4 Stabilizing Software Quality Requirements

Even in a software development "wonderland," where all functional requirements are valid, complete, and frozen before any development starts, the quality requirements would be in a far from wondrous state. As we discussed in Section 2.2.1.2, the nature of quality requirements is complex not only from the static structural point of view but also from the dynamic temporal perspective. Figure 2.24, presenting a high-level static structure of quality requirements, indicates that some of requirements can be identified explicitly through cooperation with the user/customer, while the others are the derivatives to be sought through the application of proper quality models and techniques of breaking into component parts related to these models. Although it sounds reliable, this formula applied alone will unfortunately not render the complete and fully usable set of requirements.

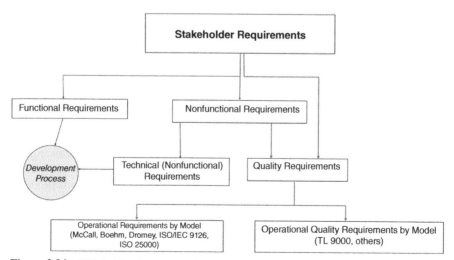

Figure 2.24   High-level static structure of quality requirements.

To understand why, let us create a little experiment. If our quality structure is based on the model from ISO/IEC 9126 (i.e., internal, external, and quality in use) and our project is in the phase of requirements definition, can we obtain useful and usable answers to the following, quality-related questions:

- What would be the level of the functional implementation completeness acceptable to the user? (A quality attribute from internal quality.)
- What level of restoration effectiveness would the customer consider satisfying? (A quality attribute from external quality.)
- What would be the mean response (task execution) time the user would be willing to accept as satisfying? (A quality attribute from external quality.)

In all three cases the answer to our principal question is negative. The reasons can be classified as follows:

- Educational. It is very probable that our interlocutor will have no adequate knowledge to deal with subject of the asked questions.
- Technical. The subjects of the questions are far too technically detailed to be addressed without a considerable amount of additional data obtained prior to any attempt to answer them.
- Temporal. The required additional data previously mentioned is physically unavailable in this phase of the project.

As a conclusion, one has to face a hard fact: completing the definition of quality requirements requires an additional elicitation effort further down in the development process. In this effort, a quality engineer will have to investigate the technical elements of the design, construction, and tests in order to obtain the missing data that will help to identify *remaining* and interrelate *all* quality requirements from different levels of technical complexity and further specify the details requested for their implementation (Fig. 2.25).

Stabilizing requirements produced through such a complicated process already seems difficult, but the level of difficulty will rise again when we analyze the complexity of interactions (and particular interests related to them) a quality engineer has to deal with in the whole process. To illustrate this complexity we will analyze the diagram presented in Fig. 2.26.

At the very beginning of the whole process a quality engineer may, should, or shall have direct interactions with representatives of the customer and his or her own organization on both higher technical and nontechnical levels. Every one of those participants will have his or her particular objectives strongly influencing the overall view of the quality. In simplified terms, a nontechnical user will seek quality elements supporting his or her core business, while a technical user will be interested more in seamless and flawless maintenance, and both most likely will try to get all of this with a minimal budget. Technical and nontechnical analysts will rely on the quality engineer in identifying and defining any and all of quality requirements that may emerge, trying at the same time to obtain as much of a budget as possible. In the case of strong limitations of the budget, the quality-related issues

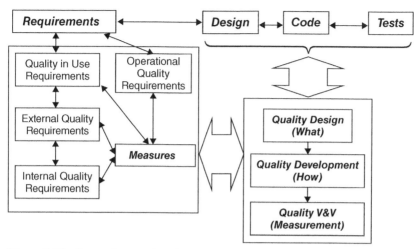

Figure 2.25   Temporal perspective of quality requirements.

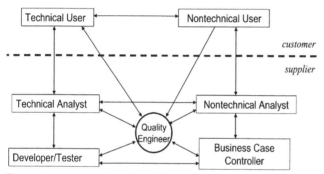

Figure 2.26   Interactions of a quality engineer in the process of quality requirements definition.

may become a hard nut to crack, for the "feature aspect" will start to fight for upper hand.

Further in the process, the principal players with whom the quality engineer will interact are still the analysts, then developers and testers and, last but not least, a business case controller. The analysts will be interfaced in further definition of higher-level quality requirements and their preliminary break down while the inter-action with developers will be needed to define mid- and low-level (technical) quality requirements. The interventions of business case controller should be (unfortunately) expected whenever a budget-related issue emerges. As reality shows, the first area considered for possible budget cuts is often quality.

We may say now that, in a nutshell, the stabilization of quality requirements depends on:

• Business expertise and eventual technical proficiency of the representatives of the customer. The higher both of them are, the better the chances for reach-ing stable cooperation and efficient exchange of information.

- Professional expertise of supplier's technical and nontechnical specialists. The higher both of them are, the bigger the chance for lasting validity of existing quality requirements.
- Technical and analytical professionalism and negotiation skills of the quality engineer.
- Maturity and quality of supplier's internal processes. Internal processes may facilitate or kill the internal cooperation and as a result influence the efficiency of engineering quality into the product.
- Completeness and stability of functional requirements, as they are strongly related to quality requirements.
- Quality of high- and low-level design, as both are required to further specify related quality requirements.
- Completeness and quality of the design of tests with which quality measurements and verification should (will) be merged.

These points make just a short list of the most important issues that the quality engineer could take into account when trying to reach some stability in his area of expertise and responsibility. It has, however, to be firmly stated that the reality of defining quality requirements may and probably will require much wider actions before these requirements may be considered "frozen."

2.2.1.5 *Quality of Quality Requirements*

The very basic set of attributes describing quality of any type of requirements has been known for decades now, and can be expressed through the following criteria:

- Correct
- Coherent
- Complete
- Feasible
- Necessary
- Verifiable
- Traceable.

In this regard quality requirements are not different from the others, however their specificity demands further discussion. One of possible ways of specifying quality of quality requirements is to evaluate them through the application of conformance conditions defined in the international standard ISO/IEC 25030—Software Engineering: Software Product Quality Requirements and Evaluation (SQuaRE)—Quality Requirements [38].

In essence, ISO/IEC 25030 identifies the set of conditions to be satisfied in order to obtain valid and robust quality requirements. After these conditions, the requirements should:

- Be uniquely identified
- Be traceable to stakeholder requirements
- Take all relevant stakeholder quality requirements into consideration
- Be associated with a chosen quality model. If the model is ISO/IEC 9126 or ISO/IEC 25010, software quality requirements should be categorized as:
  - quality in use requirements,
  - external/dynamic quality requirements, or
  - internal/static quality requirements
- Be specified in terms of a software quality measure and associated target value
- Have identified clear relations between required functions of the software and quality requirements applicable to them
- Have known criteria applied for selecting quality measures
- Have identified acceptable tolerances of target values, and
- Be linked logically and functionally to the operational profile (also known as context of use).

There are practical considerations that could be recommended to allow for further improvements of quality of requirements. One of them is developing and maintaining a list of quality measures being used, which, after certain time of accumulation, would create a rich and reliable experience base.

Another important point in obtaining quality of requirements is making them verifiable. Any requirement that cannot be objectively proven satisfied (or to the contrary) is in fact a void statement, which in turn invokes a condition that they be defined in measurable terms.

The identified requirements, even if correct and verifiable, may stay in conflict. In order to understand the nature of such a conflict and to find its solution (if it exists), an understanding of the underlying quality model is often mandatory. There are practical data indicating that, for example, a high reliability requirement, a high maintainability requirement, and a high efficiency requirement may be difficult to implement simultaneously. Solving identified conflicts between quality requirements may call for adding new or changing existing requirements. These interventions should be traceable to original quality requirements or the project will run very quickly into serious trouble.

Quality requirements should also be reviewed and approved. This particular condition refers to both validation and commitment, as on one hand quality requirements may be part of a contractual agreement so we want them to be those we all find important, feasible, and pertinent, and on the other hand it is wise to have decision makers and purse keepers consciously on our side. Also, the approval of quality requirements by the developing organization implies that the organization has the ability (technically, managerially, and financially) to meet these requirements.

Last but not least, quality requirements should be documented in a format that not only allows for free and effective discussions with participants of different levels of technical proficiency, but also makes them manageable by (or in) a configuration and change management system.

2.2.1.6   SOQUAREM: The Method for Software Quality Requirements Engineering

The IT industry needs reliable data about quality requirements to adequately evaluate systems and their architecture. The task is not easy due to nature of these requirements and the fact that existing quality requirements management methods usually deal either with one quality requirement aspect (e.g., formal design analysis framework [FDAF] for security or performance aspect [39–42]) or were developed for a specific type of software (e.g., embedded software). There is, however, a common key question related to all these methods: How does one identify quality requirements from the original source requirements of a system, user, and business? This step seems to be often simplified or bypassed by simple interviews or questionnaires, but experience shows that this is a fundamental task required to ensure the correct, operational, and properly detailed definition of quality attributes. The other very important condition often overlooked when quality requirements subject is discussed is their traceability to business requirements (discussed more in detail in Section 2.2.5). In strict business terms, anything untraceable to business goals (needs, requirements) is done for free. And that is the very basic hypothesis lying at the foundations of the SOQUAREM method.

Quality requirements emerged in the two last decades as the result of evolving technology and the increasing need for higher-quality software. The importance of quality requirements was "discovered" when software developers were faced with returned software and unsatisfied users. Problems of maintenance and costs forced the software engineering community to put emphasis on these requirements and develop quality requirements management methods. Business goal-oriented methods such as MOQARE (Misuse Oriented Quality Requirements Engineering) [43, 44] and ATAM (Architecture Tradeoff Analysis Method) [45] use business goals as main drivers in the software quality engineering process. MOQARE is based on a very interesting concept of *misuse*, where quality requirements are sought in the context of a threat to a given quality attribute and in consequence, the greatest amount of damage they may invoke if not satisfied. The method is applicable to quality requirements derived from business goals, however, due to its complexity, it may be difficult to be used in a fast-paced industrial environment. ATAM, developed by Software Engineering Institute of Carnegie Mellon University, supports evaluation of given architectural alternatives with respect to quality requirements (attributes) and identification of tradeoffs and sensitive risks early in the development process. The method focuses principally on eliciting architecture-centered quality attributes at the architectural level and offers a detailed description of quality scenario concepts, utility trees, and architectural styles, but there is no visible passage to quality requirements and measures necessary in further phases of a system life cycle. Goal-oriented methods such as ASPIRE [46] use goal graph structure as driving force to elicit and refine nonfunctional requirements. The method is a structured process for eliciting complete and measurable instances of quality attributes and is dedicated to embedded systems. In the ASPIRE approach, the quality goals are not derived from business goals and the tailoring stage is not supported by context-rich scenarios. The Soft Goal Notation approach [47, 48] is applicable to all types of quality requirements, but it is focused on the documentation and negotiation of quality requirements, not on their elicitation and traceability to business goals. Aspect-oriented methods such as FDAF are based on an *aspect-oriented paradigm* concept to define quality attributes and aspects that cannot be described in the real time version of unified modeling language (UML). FDAF framework proposes the extensions to UML notation but offers no support to identification, representation, or documentation problems at the requirements level.

Summarizing, some most important limitations of existing quality requirements management methods would be:

- Lack of processes and models describing identification, break down, and representation of quality requirements
- Lack of structured methods or techniques to identify quality requirements.

In fact, the majority of the discussed methods deal only partially or not at all with criteria related to identification, decomposition, representation, conflict analysis, documentation, and derivation of quality attributes from business goals, and so on. For example:

- None of the methods fully supports the identification of quality requirements
- Most of the methods are not based on a recognized, with international consensus, quality standard (such as ISO/IEC 9126 or ISO/IEC 25000)
- ASPIRE does not take into account the concept of business goals
- MOQARE and ATAM do not take into account the concept of quality standard and the task of quality integration with functional requirements
- MOQARE does not take into account the task of conflict analysis.

The Software Quality Requirements Engineering Method, or *SOQUAREM* [49, 50], has been developed as the response to these concerns, attempting to deliver support to systematic identification of quality requirements at the definition phase of the software development life cycle and their further transition to measureable and verifiable quality characteristics.

Dedicated to address all types of quality requirements, it is based on business context elements, scenario concepts and, at the time of development, on ISO/IEC 9126 standard to infer the related quality attributes. Business goals are main drivers of the SOQUAREM process. They are identified by applying two business-related concepts, the Business Motivation Model (BMM) and Business Context Table (BCT), used as starting points in the derivation process to identify quality requirements and deliver detailed quality attributes. Traceability of these requirements to their original source is modeled in a utility tree.

Introduced by the Business Rules Group [51], the BMM is designed to "provide a structure for developing, managing, and communicating business plans in an organized manner." It has been proposed by the Object Management Group as a simple and compact standard that provides a metamodel for enterprise-specific motivation models.

Business Context Table (BCT) describes fundamental questions about elements of business context. It structures and details items of BMM business context according to the following keyword questions: how, what, why, and who.

A utility tree links (traces) every identified and classified "necessary" quality attribute to its originating business goal. It is structured in three levels:

- Business level: where stated business goals and their refined business goals are represented. Priority of the related refined business goal is also represented.
- Quality attributes level: where derived quality attributes are represented from detailed business goals. The actor responsible for achieving quality attribute is also represented at this level.
- Scenarios level: where the meaning and role of derived quality attributes are detailed with (use case) scenarios.

SOQUAREM, being the business goals-centric, stakeholder-centered and scenarios-oriented method, is organized around two levels (Fig. 2.27):

- The business goals level, which consists of:
  - identifying important business goals from BMM and BCT
  - specific rules that are to be used to refine business goals
  - consensus and free dialogue sessions used to confirm the refined business goals with stakeholders and domain experts
- The system quality attributes level, where:
  - quality attributes are derived from the business goals according to the quality standard ISO/IEC 9126 and linkage rules
  - quality attributes are operationalized by using the scenarios template
  - quality attributes scenarios are analyzed for possible conflicts and consolidated by using prioritizing techniques
  - consensus sessions are used to confirm quality attributes scenarios with stakeholders
  - utility tree describing traceability of quality attributes is produced
- quality attributes are linked to use case model by using mapping rules.

Figure 2.28 presents key concepts involved in the main activities of SOQUA-REM process. The first activity related to *identifying and refining business goals* uses the concepts of BMM, BCT, free dialogue session, consensus session and statement, and refinement rules. The next activity, addressing *derivation of quality attributes* from the refined business goals, applies BMM and BCT, quality scenarios description, quality standard ISO/IEC 9126, linkage rules, consensus session, and

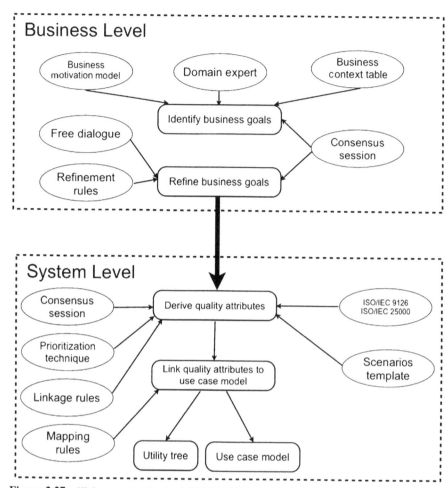

Figure 2.27   High conceptual levels of SOQUAREM.

prioritizing techniques. Two last activities, dealing with *documentation and representation of quality attributes*, use quality attributes template and utility tree.

The SOQUAREM structure is organized in steps and uses various techniques and tools (such as heuristics, mathematical and intuitive modeling, and catalogs of nonfunctional requirements methods inherited from the soft goal notation), quality standards, and verification rules. Stakeholders and domain experts are involved during process operation. Techniques used are either informal, heuristic, or semiformal. The informal ones are consensus, free dialogue session, scenario descriptions, and template. Scenario descriptions are used to detail the meaning of quality attributes and make them operational. Heuristic techniques use descriptive methods to help clarify the business goals and identify quality attributes. Semiformal methods

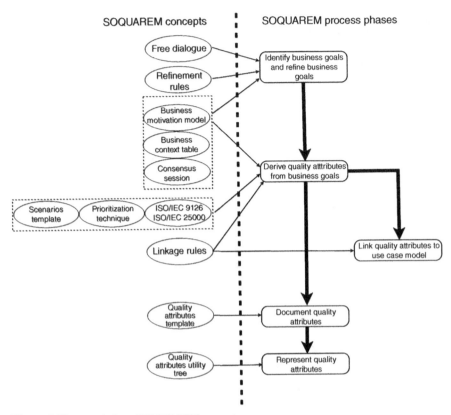

Figure 2.28   Description of SOQUAREM concepts.

use UML modeling to represent the operational parts of the quality attribute (actions undertaken to achieve it) and to link them to the functional requirements (represented in the use case model). Mathematical methods, such as as utility tree, impact matrix, and weighted methods, are used to represent quality attributes and resolve conflicts among them. Verification rules are used during the whole process to regulate the operation process and are subdivided into: statement rules to define business goals, refinement rules to refine business goals into refined business goals, linkage rules to derive quality attributes from business goals, and mapping rules to link quality attributes to the functional process by the use case model.

The SOQUAREM process model is divided into six conceptual steps for defining and refining business goals, deriving, operationalizing, analyzing, documenting, and representing quality attributes and finally for linking quality attributes to the functional process. These steps use various quality requirements elicitation techniques (questionnaire, consensus session, BMM, scenarios, prioritization, utility tree, and templates). Potential inputs of the process are BMM, BCT, and domain experts. Main participants are quality engineer, domain experts and selected stakeholders.

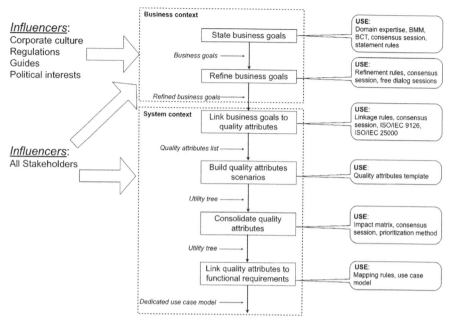

Figure 2.29   SOQUAREM process model.

SOQUAREM process model (Fig. 2.29) is represented as:

Step 1: State and identify the business goals: define relevant elements of business context such as business goals and business domain.

Step 2: Refine business goals: business goals are detailed according to additional business information such as organizational culture, regulations and guidelines, technological constraints, and business strategies to achieve business goals.

Step 3: Link business goals to the corresponding quality attributes: detailed business goals are used to derive the quality attributes by using ISO/IEC 9126 quality standard and linkage rules.

Step 4: Build quality attributes scenarios by using the scenarios template and the consensus session techniques to infer the right quality attributes.

Step 5: Analyze conflicts among QAs and consolidate them by using prioritization methods.

Step 6: Link quality attributes to the functional requirements process by updating the initial use case model with additional information about QAs.

As illustrated by Fig. 2.30, in the logic of the SOQUAREM process model, quality attributes are identified from business goals with elements of business context such as BMM and BCT being used to help identify them and further refine them into refined business goals. Later, quality attributes are linked to refined business

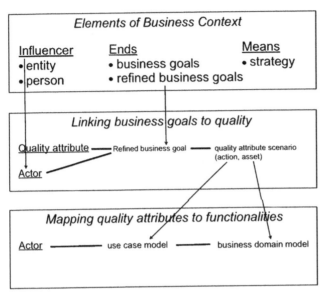

Figure 2.30   Logic of SOQUAREM process model.

goals by using scenarios and quality standard ISO/IEC 9126. They are also integrated into the functional process by means of mapping rules, use cases, and business domain models. Traceability from business requirements to system specifications is realized by mapping business context elements to quality attributes of system level in two ways:

- Business goals are refined into sub goals and linked to quality attributes
- Influencers (external and internal) are mapped to actors responsible for achieving quality attribute.

The main objective of the SOQUAREM process is to build a bridge between business level elements and system level ones and allow more interaction between stakeholders, software people, and domain experts during consensus and free dialogue sessions.

There are some interesting aspects differentiating SOQUAREM from other existing methods that deserve attention:

- More interaction with stakeholders and domain experts during consensus and free dialogue sessions
- Use of intuitive modeling and motivation of business in the derivation process of quality attributes
- Structured derivation of quality goals from business goals by using BCT and BMM)

- Derivation step of quality attributes from business goals is fully described in SOQUAREM
- Use of scenarios at the requirements level to resolve terminology problems and infer the correct quality attributes
- Use of verification rules such as statement rules to define business goals, refinement rules to refine business goals, linkage rules to derive quality attributes from business goals, and mapping rules to link quality attributes to the FRs model
- Use of globally recognized ISO/IEC 9126 as quality standard for SOQUAREM process
- Use of quality template to specify and document quality attributes
- Use of prioritizing methods (impact matrix and weighted method) to resolve conflicts among quality attributes.

In its standard-related part, SOQUAREM refers to ISO/IEC 9126, but as this standard slowly becomes obsolete and is being gradually replaced by the documents from ISO/IEC 25000 series, the updated version of the method should be expected to be publicly available soon.

2.2.2 Software Quality Design

The leading idea that software quality engineering is an effort similar to that of software development implies that quality itself is a "product" being subject to interventions if not identical to then at least resembling those from the development process. In the previous chapter we discussed the first of them, quality requirements definition and specification, indicating where and in what this activity differs from classic functional requirements specification. The next logical step is then the *design* of quality. This subject will be discussed in a close relationship with system design efforts.

2.2.2.1 What Is the Design of Quality?

Quality design is the phase in which the quality engineer translates quality requirements gathered earlier into his or her technical representations (or, in simpler form, executable to-dos) applicable in the next phases. But unfortunately it is not so simple. The results of the quality design process also have to be:

- Applicable immediately in the software/system design phase, no matter the development model chosen
- Further refined and complemented to descend to the level required in a construction phase.

To explain this idea, let us analyze the situation presented in Fig. 2.31, where two processes, system and quality engineering, meet in their respective design phases.

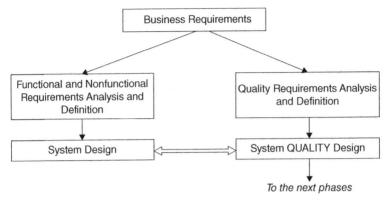

Figure 2.31 System and quality design interaction.

System design, following the convention proposed in Reference 1, is an activity that aims "to determine a set of components and inter-component interfaces that satisfy a specified set of requirements." The following important keywords (and their respective notions) can be withdrawn from the above statement:

- System. This keyword has a connotation of a *complete*, functioning entity, seen through its externally observable behavior.
- Decomposition. The process of "dismantling" the one complex solution into a set of interrelated smaller but simpler subsolutions (components).
- Component. A functional *smaller* entity, subsystem, or piece of software that together with the other components shall constitute a system.
- Inter-component interfaces. For the sake of our analysis, the word *interactions* would be preferable as wider. The interactions make the real bloodstream of a system, through which the components communicate.

When analyzing these notions one can easily notice that all four of them have strong quality dependences. Our *system* may or may not exhibit requested quality; the *decomposition* that leads to architecture may but does not have to automatically have the quality high; the *components*, similarly to the system, may be of low or high quality; and finally the *interactions* are also subject to such an evaluation. In this sense the design of quality means identifying, specifying, and indicating to the development team all quality-related to-dos that should be taken care of in the system design phase. To see it clearer let us imagine a fictitious discussion between a quality engineer (Bob) and an architect (Frank):

    Bob: From my quality requirements definition phase I have identified the following, system-level quality attributes: system availability has to be minimum 98%, the mean recovery time should not exceed 1 min/failure and the customer requests that the relative user efficiency be at least 0.9.

    Frank: Well, it sounds okay, but what I am supposed to do with it?

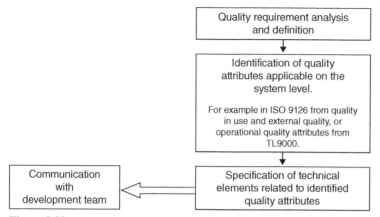

Figure 2.32 Engineering process for introducing quality into system design.

Bob: These attributes have the following impact on your design: the availability
of 98% means that the system must be available 59 minutes out of every
operational hour at any time, so your design should strive to exhibit high
reliability. One of the options you may take into account is using stable
technologies and enhanced application of reuse. The recovery time below
1 min/failure may request applying super efficient recovery algorithms
together with extra fast hardware. Finally, user efficiency of 0.9 and above
translates into such a functional user interface and online help design that
there will be virtually no difference in operation between and average
user and an expert.

This example illustrates the way in which system and quality engineering could
interact to build a quality product from very beginning. To systematize this direction
of the cooperation one should proceed as shown in Fig. 2.32.

   As it has been stated in sections discussing requirement definition, it is a rare
situation where all quality requirements are complete before reaching the phase of
construction. The main reason for such a situation is missing data. The design phase
is the first place where existing quality requirements can be verified and eventually
modified if necessary, but first and foremost they can be developed to the level that
will allow for completing quality design, which, among others, means *building the
personalized quality model*. The first part of the process allowing for reaching this
stage is shown in Fig. 2.33.

   The system-level quality design may require several iterations before it reaches
its complete and stable state. As can be seen in Fig. 2.33, these iterations are wide
in a sense that they also run through system design process. The logic of such an
approach is the following:

- Quality-related technical elements introduced into the system design (arrow,
  A) may induce changes in the design itself. Even if not, in a professional

practice the whole design always goes through the verification and validation process.

- The results of verification and validation of the design will be used to *update* the corresponding design of quality (arrow B). Updating means both adjusting the already existing design *and* adding the elements that resulted from the system design. This part is crucial for finalizing quality design.

- The updated quality design should go through its own verification and validation process. Its results may require another intervention on the level of system design (arrow A).

- And so on until both designs are verified, validated, as complete as possible in their actual reality, and *corresponding*.

The principal exchange of data allowing for effective system and quality design runs through channels represented by arrows A and B. The functioning of the channel A has been illustrated earlier in this section in the form of the discussion between a quality engineer Bob and his system counterpart, Frank. To illustrate channel B we will use the same formula, except this time the discussion will be originated by Frank (system design side).

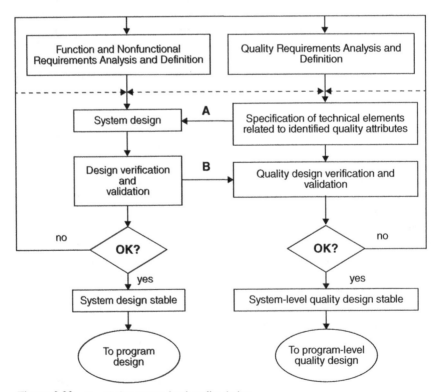

Figure 2.33 Completing system-level quality design.

Frank: When designing our system I have learned that the chances for reuse are slim at best as the system is rather new, that some of core services of the system cannot be developed without applying the latest 5G (fifth generation) tools and that in order to keep the mean recovery time not exceeding 1 min/failure I will have to use the newest hardware, not yet matured in large public use.

Bob: These decisions may have some impact on quality design. They will have to be analyzed further, but as for now I can indicate the following: the requirement of 98% availability may not be possible to fulfill as the technology to be used is not stable enough. This requirement will have to be redefined and most probably renegotiated. Applying hardware not yet matured in large public use invokes the issue of user's safety. The minimal safety level requested in our sector of operation is X, and your design will have to comply with it. After verifying and validating these new aspects I will return to you with updated quality-related technical elements.

What happened during this discussion is the *update* of quality design that follows the impact of the constraints applied to the system design. Applying the most modern technology, inevitable if we want to satisfy core functional requirements, invokes an elevated risk and in turn may make unrealistic 98% availability. This will have to be reconsidered on all levels, from technical to business. Using hardware that has not yet matured in a large public use introduces a new quality aspect and its related requirement, safety, which would probably not have emerged had the hardware been mature. Finally, the validation and verification that is required in order to update the quality design opens a new iteration leading hopefully to a better quality of the system.

The next step of quality design is the design of program quality. The process of the design is similar to this on system level (Fig. 2.34), except program design applies principally to code and its related documentation, or in other words to static artifacts of the development. What is important to note is the fact that program quality design inherits from system quality design. In simpler terms, the code must possess such quality attributes that, when composed together, will make the whole system satisfy the quality requirements.

To understand it better let us take an example based on the ISO 9126 quality model and measures. If a system-level quality attribute (or a subcharacteristic, as it is termed in ISO 9126) from the external quality category is *interoperability*, which implies that the system should be able to effectively communicate with the external world, then the program-level quality attribute should be sought in the internal quality category and have interoperability connotations. In the case of ISO 9126, this internal quality subcharacteristic is also *interoperability*, and implies that the program should be able to communicate effectively with *its* external world. Such an inheritance is relatively easy to follow and applies in quality design in the case of the external–internal quality relationship within ISO 9126 (both categories share the same quality model); however, it will not be helpful when program quality design

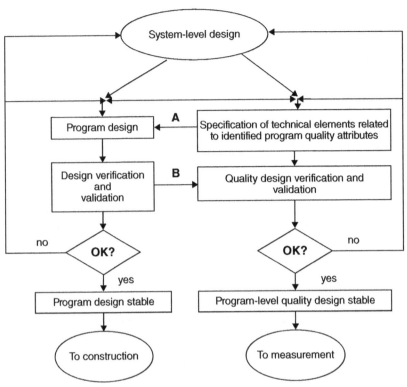

Figure 2.34   Completing program-level quality design.

must subdue to quality in use attributes. The only link between quality in use and program quality is logic of consequences. For example, the quality in use attribute *economic productivity* cannot be linked in any automated way to any program quality (internal quality) attributes, but intuitively we know that a system built from badly designed and coded program modules will most probably be slow, ineffective, and failure-prone, which in turn will prohibit any productivity from happening.

The step of quality design allowing for the real control of the engineering results is the choice (identification and rationale) of measures that should be taken in order to evaluate the quality of developed system and the assignment of target values against which the measurement results will be compared. It is obvious that these measures are direct logical descendants of the design, but the choice once again is not automatic. ISO/IEC 9126, for example, contains over 200 measures associated with its quality model characteristics and subcharacteristics, and it is difficult to imagine all of them classified "indispensable" and even more difficult to see them all taken without creating serious bottlenecks in the project. The same limitation applies to quality attributes (characteristics and subcharacteristics) constituting our design of quality. We will rarely, if ever, be interested in all possible quality attributes from the quality model we chose for our project. So, on the level of quality

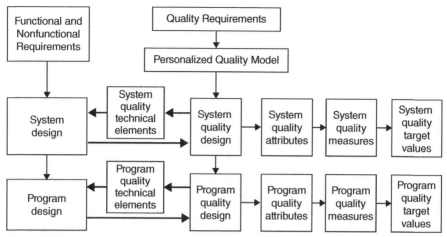

Figure 2.35   Personalized quality implementation map.

design, we also choose what is most important to obtain and what is less important, creating, as has already been mentioned, the quality model personalized for our project. This leads us back to the question asked in the title of this section: What is quality design?

To answer this question we will introduce a concept of *personalized quality implementation map*. As on the real, geographic map, we will find there the information required to get to the point of our destination, except instead of having full content, we will only have what is needed in our trip. The *personalized quality implementation map* in its basic form contains (Fig. 2.35):

- Quality requirements for the developed system
- A project-personalized quality model resulting from quality requirements
- Quality attributes descending from the quality model
- Quality-related technical elements (development to-dos) corresponding to quality attributes
- Quality measures linked to quality attributes
- Target values mapped to quality measures.

To make the *map* and the quality design complete some complementary elements should be added:

- Quality measurement process, planning, and methods
- Quality evaluation process, planning, and methods
- Evaluation results analysis and interpretation methods
- Methods, planning, and criteria for evaluation of the quality of accompanying documentation and services
- Tools.

Once such a map is properly constructed, a quality engineer has all the required tools (and also some decisive power) to effectively participate in a creation of a "blue screen-free" and professional software system.

It can be noticed that the procedures applied in quality design in consecutive phases of the system (or software) life cycle look similar. In fact, they follow a common process and use the common set of normative support documents (of the choice of the designer). Figure 2.36 presents a generic model of a quality design process that can be easily used by quality designers when passing from one phase of the life cycle to the next.

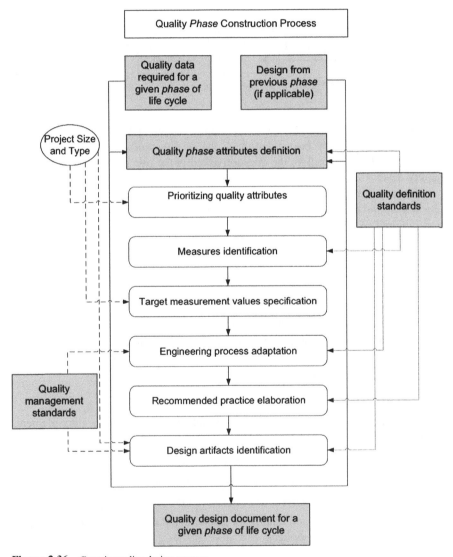

Figure 2.36   Generic quality design process.

Of course, the model is applicable only in the phases that are either purely of the design nature (architectural design, program design) or at least have some design notion in them (requirements definition, construction). To use this generic process, the designer has to fill up a few introductory blanks in the model. And so:

- *Phase* has to be replaced by the real phase of the life cycle in which the design shall take place. Example: program design phase.

- *Quality data* required for a given phase of life cycle have to be replaced by input data from the previous phase. Example: quality in use requirements as input data for system design phase.

- *Quality definition standards* should be chosen according to the phase in which design is to take place. Example: ISO/IEC 9126-4 or ISO/IEC 25022 when quality in use is the subject.

The last general comment concerning the design of quality would be as follows: in a real industrial environment there usually is no time for elaborate exercises of developing proprietary quality models and measures. It is then recommended and helpful to use as much as possible what is already developed, taking into account the simple fact that designing a very good meal is faster and more secure with a menu in hand than when doing it from scratch, especially when the menu is graced by a large, possibly international consensus.

The example of using ISO/IEC 9126 as a quality design *menu* illustrates this approach with one important correction: it should be replaced by the ISO/IEC 25000 SQuaRE series the first moment the standards are fully published.

2.2.2.2 Practical Aspects of Designing Quality into a Software Product

Quality design, similarly to any design effort, depends on requirements and their completeness, feasibility, and quality. Having said so, we can identify the first practical aspect of quality design as the validation of requirements coming to us. It would be prudent to discuss the actual set of quality requirements with analysts and designers in order to obtain their early, technically oriented feedback before actually any design begins. Such a consultation may prove fruitful for all involved if we keep in mind the mutual influence of both designs. This recommendation holds its value further down the development process, when we repeat similar activities applied to program (quality) design.

Another important practical aspect of quality design is its testability, understood as the basis for developing early test scenarios. For example, the quality attribute "recoverability" implies the existence of mechanisms, both soft and hard, that, when implemented, will satisfy the need of the particular level of recoverability. It is then possible in the design stage to identify a scenario or scenarios in which we will check how the system behaves after the failure, define the stimuli used to provoke failures, and even classify/prioritize the types of failures we would be interested in.

Quality design neither is nor should be executed without some kind of structural foundations making a framework for the overall effort. Usually as such a framework we explore quality models; however, the practical aspect of this point is *measures*.

One could ask the very valid question of why the models from ISO/IEC 9126 and ISO/IEC 25010 are *so* recommended. Are they really the best we could lay our hands on? This book is not the place to offer such an ultimate opinion, but what surely may be said is that these models come with measures. Again, we may divagate whether these measures are the best or not, but at least the quality engineer is not left empty-handed. The decision of applying other existing models or even of developing our own quality model will inevitably invoke the need for designing the measures and associated with them methods of evaluation, analysis and interpretation.

This may be considered a valid option (see Reference 52), but here again is a catch. As long as such a custom method is used for internal, organization-proprietary purposes all may work smoothly and effectively, but the complications begin when we have to prove to the external evaluator (e.g., a user) that the quality actually is there. Using a home-cooked method will rarely allow for market-recognized certification (like that of ISO 9001) and as the result the effort may undergo a painful process of individual, often external verification.

Some of the biggest challenges in system and quality engineering are the integration procedures describing the way in which both efforts should melt into a coherent and effective process. Depending on individual policies applied in organizations, these procedures may be more or less structured or disciplined, but all that will boil down to three key elements: team structure, overlapping of knowledge, and decisional power distribution. The development team that has no position reserved for a quality engineer will be given the "quality-refusal" option, or, in other words, the option of pushing aside quality aspects as "less important now." The overlapping of knowledge is a communication bridge between those who build and those whose job is to help the builders do so well. The very basic knowledge of quality engineering notions should then be a part of the expertise required from developers, while a good, working knowledge of the largely understood development subject is indispensable in the expertise of a quality engineer. Last but surely not least is the distribution of the decisional power within the development team. The quality engineer having no power to influence the development effort when he can prove it justifiable is a risky concept and an unforgivable waste of resources and budget. By definition the quality engineer is there to help in making things better and making better things, and positioning him or her as a powerless consultant will bring no considerable profits, especially in the industrial environment, where the biggest pressure is time to market and quality reflections often come too late, after the client starts complaining.

2.2.2.3   *Planning the Quality Verification*

We have already stated that the effectiveness of quality engineering hides in the ability to measure it and verify its compliance to requirements. Verifying whether quality is actually there requires a specific approach that we can call a dual (or *bifocal*) perspective. This dualism comes from the following idea: the final quality of the system results from quality *in* the phase and quality *of* the phase. Quality *in* the phase is what we called an executable to-do, which, when executed, should bring required quality attributes to the system. Quality *of* the phase is a feature that says whether the phase itself has been done properly. Let us look at the following simple example: the design of a given system contains all required functions and functionalities, but the design itself is, for lack of a less deprecating word, "fuzzy." What are the chances that the system developed following such a design will nevertheless exhibit the required quality? Let us say "some," but surely smaller than when a system follows a clear, disciplined, and well-documented design. This applies equally well to the design of quality itself and will be briefly discussed in the next chapter.

The two aspects of quality discussed here should be reflected in quality verification and its planning together with their feasibility (or actual place within the development cycle where the physical verification can take place). Instinctively we know that the quality *of* the phase has to be verified in course of this phase, so its planning has to be synchronized with the phase's advancement, processes, and produced artifacts. Things get more complicated when we should plan the verification of the quality *in* the phase. Let us recall again the example from Section 2.2.2.1:

> *Bob:* From my quality requirements definition phase I have identified the following, system-level quality attributes: system availability has to be minimum 98%, the mean recovery time should not exceed 1 min/failure and the customer requests that the relative user efficiency be at least 0.9.

The executable to-dos indicated in this example cannot be verified in the design phase, as they require a running system to be measured, evaluated, and validated. A similar situation will take place on any level of the design, be it business-related or code-related: the verification of quality will require the existence of related artifacts or all the effort is just another theoretical experiment of no larger, tangible value. To help better grasp the importance of this statement, one can observe the approach presented in Fig. 2.37, which, in a somehow simplified way, illustrates the method we could use when planning quality verification.

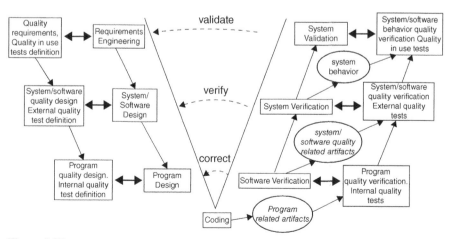

Figure 2.37 Planning quality verification.

In case of the V-model from Fig. 2.37, the first product-related artifacts begin to appear during coding (we do not take into account an accelerated development of user documentation that in some cases can be undertaken) to further evolve into system-related artifacts. Knowing the development model used in a particular project, a quality engineer can, relatively early in the process, identify the moments and places within the development cycle (sometimes with precision to real calendar dates) where the artifacts required for quality verification will appear. This knowledge should allow for creating a feasible verification plan containing at least the following elements:

- Measurement plan defining when and where the measurements will be taken
- The overall schedule
- Required human resources
- Tools and environment
- Budget
- Temporal distribution of usage of both human and material resources
- Changes and iterations management.

This content is merely a framework of what can be created in real situations, which means that the organization caring for the quality of its product may build a quality verification plan that is much more elaborate, detailed, and rich but, again, it all will boil down to corporate policy- and budget-based quality objectives, long and short-term plans and decisions.

2.2.2.4 *Quality of Quality Design*
Quality of quality design is just a question about how well the design itself was done.

Before discussing the subject, let's quickly recapitulate quality design product, the personalized quality implementation map. The *personalized quality implementation map* basically covers:

- Quality requirements for the developed system
- The project-personalized quality model resulting from quality requirements
- Quality attributes descending from the quality model
- Quality-related technical elements (development to-dos) corresponding to quality attributes
- Quality measures linked to quality attributes
- Target values mapped to quality measures.

The *map*, in order to be realizable, has to be accompanied by quality measurement, evaluation, results analysis and interpretation processes, planning and methods, and adequate tools and documentation. So what could go wrong? Pretty much anything.

The very basic set of attributes describing the quality of requirements can also be almost unchanged when applied in verification of the quality of the quality design, and can be expressed through asking the following questions: Is the design:

- Correct?
- Coherent?
- Complete?
- Feasible?
- Verifiable?
- Maintainable?
- Traceable?

A *correct* and *complete* quality design produces the *personalized quality implementation map* that properly addresses all identified quality requirements, and links them to development artifacts on one hand and to the model and applicable measures on the other. Finally, such a design correctly translates quality requirements and attributes into engineering "to-dos" (objectives and tasks) that can be communicated to, understood by, and executed by technical professionals.

A *coherent* quality design is not only easy to follow and understand, but also follows the logical pattern recognized within the project. The very basis for obtaining that coherence of the quality design is the application of a stable, logical quality model. Once a logical transition path with clearly visible transition phases can link every requirement and the results of its implementation, the majority of the quality design coherence task is achieved.

A *feasible* quality design responds to feasible and reasonable quality requirements and produces technically feasible and financially justifiable engineering to-dos. For example, a quality in use requirement of a 250% increase of productivity may in itself be unfeasible, and, if accepted, will most probably lead to partially unfeasible quality design, where the resulting engineering effort will not be technically possible or will invoke unjustifiable costs.

A *verifiable* quality design comes with measures that not only are correct and appropriate but are also doable. While a *feasible* quality design delivers feasible engineering to-dos, a *verifiable* design goes a step further and defines the measures that are to be taken and evaluated in order to prove the correct realization of the required engineering effort. If for some reason the identified measure is impossible (cannot be taken), the part of the design related to it is unverifiable and has to be properly addressed.

A *maintainable* quality design in this regard is no different from any design or even document that will be used over time. So it has to be properly structured, if required, modularized, documented in an appropriate format, and kept under the supervision of change (or version) control tools. It also has to be modifiable without losing its clarity and full traceability to requirements.

And, last but not least, a quality design must be *traceable*. Let's recall here the basic truth of traceability in business: anything untraceable to a business goal is done for free and as such qualifies for immediate termination. A fully traceable quality design has to exhibit at least one link from any of its components to at least one business goal (objective or requirement). In simple terms, if the quality engineer presents a developer with a particular, quality-related engineering to-do that requires extra coding, he or she requires extra work that has a financial representation in overall project spending. If this to-do cannot be traced back within quality design to a given quality requirement and further to an originating business objective, this effort will be recognized as unjustified spending, booked as a potential budget loss, and immediately terminated. The Consolidated Traceability Model presented in Section 2.2.5.2 has been developed to address this concern.

2.2.3 Software Quality Engineering Implementation

Software quality engineering implementation, strategically speaking, should be a part of a bigger picture originating on a corporate strategy level. Ideally, the strategy should define the main directives for processes (such as quality assurance processes), engineering technologies and techniques, and required resources, and glue it all into one coherent mechanism, of which individual instantiations would be used in every project run by the organization. As is shown in Fig. 2.38, such an approach combines three elements: strategy, processes, and engineering. Let's analyze what happens when one or more of these elements is missing.

Missing *strategy* is a frequently observable state of small and medium companies, particularly in their start-up phase (CMMI levels 1 and 2). Quite often, quality assurance processes are not there yet too, so what are their chances of building a software or system with the required quality? Similar to those of winning the war, perhaps, but as long as they have soldiers who can use arms (engineering), they still have a chance to win the battle.

Missing *processes*, with or without strategy, surely can make things messier than required. Their lack may slow down the development, increase costs, decrease productivity, and generally do a lot of secondary harm to the project itself, but again, as long as the engineering force is there, the final product has the chances for good quality.

Missing *engineering* is like trying to win the war having a superb strategy, exceptional management and control processes, and no soldiers. There is practically no chance to build a quality product if the required quality engineering knowledge and skills are absent or too limited.

2.2.3.1 When Does the Implementation Start?

To answer this question, two different perspectives should be taken into consideration: the organization and the project.

As was shown in Fig. 2.38, the engineering could and should be rooted in and supported by an appropriate corporate strategy, so from organizational standpoint, the real quality engineering implementation begins when the organization reaches the adequate maturity level (e.g., CMMI levels 4 and 5, but sometimes level 3 is

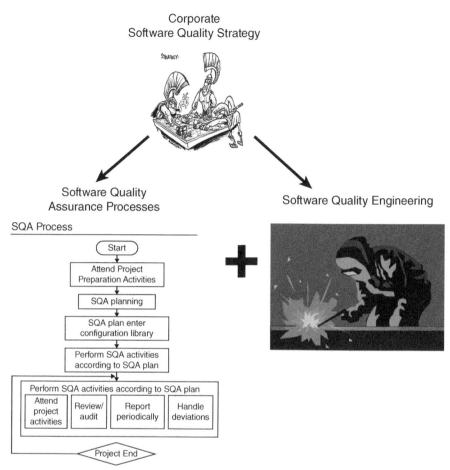

Figure 2.38   Relationship between strategy, processes, and engineering in software quality engineering.

already sufficient). On these levels, instead of being treated as purely execution-type activity applied on a project-by-project basis, quality engineering becomes a part of a longer-term strategic plan with at least technical, technological, experience accumulation and retention, and staffing perspectives taken into consideration. Also, the presence of appropriate quality assurance processes is somehow linked to the maturity of the organization and, when these processes are correct, it helps the engineering develop the product of required quality. Once these elements are taken care of, the organization can claim that in its case, the software or system quality engineering implementation is in place and operational.

From a project perspective, software quality engineering should start *immediately*, which means at the same moment when the first analysis of an opportunity begins. The reasons for this hastiness are both technological and budgetary. As was discussed in Section 1.2.1, almost every project on this planet has some budgetary constraints, within which functionality and quality have to find their proper and justified places in order to create the required final product. The sooner we begin analyzing quality needs that go with demanded functionalities, the greater are the chances that the necessary budget will be identified and, when agreed upon, correctly distributed. The feasibility constraint that is briefly discussed in the following is also linked to the budget distribution subject as, for example, for some "quality extravaganza" the requested budget may simply be too big to be accepted by the customer.

The technological reason for implementing quality engineering as early as possible goes with the question: Will it be feasible? To understand this concern, let us imagine a project where the requested functionalities invoke the application of the most recent technologies. The eventual decision of applying them may render the high *reliability* quality characteristic of the future system unfeasible from engineering point of view, as usually very new technologies are unreliable by themselves, so the products developed using them have even more chances of unsatisfactory quality.

2.2.3.2 *Quality Implementation within Development Activities*

The discussion of software quality implementation within development activities can go in different ways, depending on the choice of the system or software life cycle model [53]. In this section, the structure of the quality implementation analysis will be based on the generic model proposed in ISO/IEC 24748-1 Systems and software engineering—Guide for life cycle management [54]. Chapter 4 of the ISO/IEC 24748 standard defines six stages (or *phases*) of a generic system life cycle:

- Concept
- Development
- Production
- Utilization
- Support
- Retirement.

The software or system quality will be further represented through ISO/IEC 9126 quality model, its measures and vocabulary, as at the moment of writing this book ISO/IEC 25000 SQuaRE series is still incomplete (the standards defining measures are under development).

2.2.3.2.1 *Concept Stage*

One of the main objectives of the concept stage is to assess new business opportunities and to develop preliminary system quality requirements and a feasible design solution that meets these quality requirements.

As was discussed in Section 2.2.1, identifying quality requirements as thoroughly as possible is generally recognized as the first and most critical step in quality implementation for any project. This includes making sure that stakeholder's needs for quality are correctly and completely identified. Three categories of requirements are expected:

- Functional
- Nonfunctional
- Quality requirements.

Of course, the latter is the most important from software quality engineering perspective.

Let's recall from Section 2.1.3 that, depending of the version of quality model (ISO/IEC 9126-1 or ISO/IEC 25010), quality requirements can be further categorized as:

- Quality in use requirements
- External/dynamic quality requirements
- Internal/static quality requirements.

In case of OTS software, a fourth category of operational quality requirement could be taken into consideration.

In ISO/IEC 24784-1, the requirement analysis happens in the concept phase. At this stage, the stakeholder/user's quality needs have to be identified and elicited and will contribute to specifying quality in use requirements, operational quality requirements for OTS software, external/dynamic quality requirements, and, in rare occasions, internal/static quality requirements.

In the concept stage, as the concepts and the requirements are being developed, trade-offs between functional, nonfunctional, quality requirements, and other project constraints should be analyzed, documented, and possibly concluded. But let's again recall after Section 2.2.1: quality requirements usually are not fully defined at the end of this stage. They require further elicitation, as trade-offs between functional, nonfunctional, quality requirements, and design feasibility occur.

In this stage, a quality plan should be assembled with all quality-related activities defined, including types of reviews that should be carried out for each artifact of the project. Ideally, the quality plan should be a guide for the whole quality engineering effort throughout all following life cycle stages. The plan should additionally cover classic quality assurance (QA), traditional verification and validation (V&V), but also quality requirements analysis and design together with identification of quality engineering activities (or engineering to-dos) that should be implemented further in the system life cycle. The plan should also identify and appoint a quality engineer.

Usually, the concept stage begins with the recognition of quality needs and requirements for a new system or software, or for the modification of an existing one, so the acquirer/user's feedback to the system's concept and expected system or software quality attributes should be obtained during this activity.

One or more alternative concepts to meet the stakeholder needs or requirements should be developed, balancing functional, nonfunctional, and quality requirements.

To ensure proper coverage of the projected system's quality attributes, a quality model should be selected and further applied. Quality characteristics and subcharacteristics elicited from the model and quality requirements should be formally identified, along with selected measures to be later used in the system's quality verification and validation.

One or more support systems for designing, measuring, and evaluating quality should be identified and candidate solutions included in the evaluation of alternatives in order to arrive at a balanced and integrated solution to operate and support the system over its life cycle. A quality engineering approach should be selected, planned, and integrated onto the other project plans.

The required concept stage outcome could be listed as:

- Quality model
- Quality engineering approach
- Quality plan
- Appointed quality engineer
- Quality baseline (attributes, requirements, and selected measures for quality in use and external quality)
- Concepts (of operation, of support, etc.)
- Trade offs and other analysis results
- Quality engineer's active participation in reviews
- Quality engineer's active participation in change management
- Quality records.

2.2.3.2.2   *Development Stage*

Before beginning the architectural design, the requirements from the concept stage should be refined properly, including quality requirements. Quality in use and external quality attributes and requirements should be fully developed while internal quality attributes and requirements may still be in a drafted state. All requirements shall be "baselined," which means identified, defined, and rendered *official*. It also means that any change that may be necessary beyond this point requires a formal process of revision and acceptance.

From the perspective of quality engineering, the system or software has to be designed for quality. In other words, the developer should identify and use the proper design techniques in order to meet the quality requirements, especially those related to external quality. All quality requirements should be met by the resulting design, which also means that all elements of the design that are responsible for exhibiting required quality by the system (e.g., appropriate learnability) have to be in place in this stage. The quality engineer should be involved in this task together with the designers.

Applicable quality measures should be identified and/or developed to allow later control of the implementation of the quality requirements.

To ensure that all quality attributes were designed into a system or software and will satisfy the quality requirements, the traceability between quality requirements and design artifacts should be always observed. This traceability will help in ensuring that no requirement is accidentally overlooked and that "gold plating" with unnecessary features does not occur either.

The development stage begins with completing the elicitation of quality requirements, then a design solution is produced for the new or modified system or software. The design solution considers all requirements defined in the precedent stage and those that have been refined in this stage. The development stage also identifies quality attributes to be implemented during the production stage in the form of internal quality requirements. Applicable measures should be defined and proper mechanisms prepared to later measure and evaluate the resulting system or software.

To ensure that all requirements (functional, nonfunctional, and quality requirements) are being taken into account, traceability should be formally established and maintained. As a practical observation, not all software tools used in change control process (traceability) are ready to deal with software/system quality requirements in the same way they as they do with functional requirements.

The main objective of the development stage is to develop a system or software that meets stakeholder functional and quality requirements, and that can be produced (i.e., that is *doable*), tested, evaluated, operated, supported, and retired. The most important outcomes of the development stage are:

- Quality baseline for this stage (quality in use, external and internal quality attributes, requirements, and measures)
- Quality requirements traceability structure
- Design that meets the quality requirements
- Design that includes:
  ○ The main system or software
  ○ All supporting mechanisms (systems) required to measure and evaluate quality
- Trade offs and other analysis results
- Quality engineer's active participation in reviews
- Quality engineer's active participation in change management
- Quality records.

2.2.3.2.3   Production Stage

"Production stage" is a concise term encapsulating several phases otherwise known as *implementation, integration, verification, validation*, and *transition* in ISO/IEC 15288, or *coding, unitary tests, integration tests, system tests*, and *user tests* in the majority of popular software engineering literature. Due to its vastness, this stage shall consider the quality model selected and the complete baseline accumulated from previous stages and perform quality activities according to the plans.

System or software internal/static, external/dynamic, and quality in use should physically be implemented during this stage. Let's recall, however, what was said earlier about quality requirements: only those requirements that reflect the behavior of the software or system are related to coding (Section 1.2.1). In consequence, the production stage understood in these terms may not entirely satisfy the quality requirements related, for example, to satisfaction as the latter combines the software itself (functionality and quality) but also the quality of training, documentation, and so on.

The role of quality engineer in this stage is particularly diversified, for he or she not only should assist the developers in internal/static quality realization during coding and unitary tests, but also should actively participate in the integration process and execute appropriate quality measurements during all test phases. More precisely, quality measurement should be:

- Properly designed as quality tests
- Executed in every stage where related artifacts are produced
- As unobtrusive as possible, which means embedded into main tests.

The last point requires an additional comment. The tests are a very important but also a delicate period in the overall creation effort, so the smarter the test design, the better the overall project results. Quality requirements are for the most part linked to functionalities and their verification requires the existence of the related artifacts, but exactly the same can be said about functional requirements. So in most situations executing functional tests and quality tests separately would require instantiating the same artifact twice. In some cases it may be as trivial as pushing the "power" button, but it also can be imagined that measuring usability characteristics of a given software or system requires a running instance of this system and this may by much more complex than just pushing a button. Besides, it seems more convenient to check the *totality* of a given functionality at once and in the same usage context.

Consequently the internal, external, and early quality in use data coming from the test suites defined earlier in test plans should be stored and made part of the quality baseline. Measurement methods should follow standardized documentation linked to the chosen quality model; a quality evaluation method should be selected and executed, again, in connection with the quality model.

In order to assist the developers in obtaining the required quality during the production stage, the quality engineer should use resulting data to continuously evaluate in-production quality and communicate the obtained results and improvement recommendations to the development team. He or she should also be responsible for verification of consistency between internal/static, external/dynamic, and quality in use.

Again, a practical observation: the position of a quality engineer should be associated with the appropriate decisional influence, or all the data and all resulting recommendations will be pointless.

It is recommended that the data acquired during the production stage be further used as reference when monitoring the quality in utilization and support stages. Joint reviews for internal, external, and quality in use verification should be periodically executed to ensure compliance with requirements and, if an organization applies a quality management system, such quality records of every project should be collected.

The expected outcomes of the production stage are:

- Updated quality baseline, with
  - internal, external, and quality in use attributes, requirements and measures
  - quality evaluation plan
  - implementation quality V&V (test and measurement) results
- Quality engineer's active participation in reviews
- Quality engineer's active participation in production process
- Quality engineer's active participation in decisional process
- Quality engineer's active participation in change management
- Quality records.

2.2.3.2.4 *Utilization Stage*

The ISO/IEC 24748-1 standard serving as the framework of this chapter mentions "monitoring performance and identifying, classifying and reporting of anomalies, deficiencies, and failures" [54] as basic activities of the stage, and that requires reference data (e.g., performance targets or deficiency levels).

It seems profitable then that a defined and sound quality attributes baseline (with all required details) be used for this purpose. This baseline obviously should come as the combined result from the concept, development, and production stages, be used in the support and retirement stages, and be kept up to date during the complete life of the system or software.

The performance of the system should be monitored and incidents and problems should be managed in a formal way because they are direct contributors to the system owner/user's satisfaction. Whenever applicable, user requests (such as standard changes, help desk requests, or customer support) should also be managed because of the effect they have on user satisfaction (quality in use). All the necessary support systems required to manage quality activities such as measurement, incidents, problems, events, request, and access should be in place (if possible and feasible).

The utilization stage aims at efficiently delivering the services in accordance with targeted quality in use attributes; however, external and internal quality attributes should also be monitored, as they are direct contributors to perceived quality in use.

Anomalies, deficiencies, and failures in delivering the services should be identified, recorded, classified, reported, and acted upon, with the prime objective of restoring the services to their expected level and maximizing quality as it is perceived by the system owner/user.

As mentioned earlier, the activities in this phase should use and maintain the quality baseline (attributes, requirements, targets and selected measures, V&V data, and quality-related data) that are shared with the other phases of the system's life-cycle in order to maintain the integrity of the product and its engineering effort.

Based on all quality attributes, the qualitative retirement criteria should be established and further used to trigger the execution of the retirement stage.

The expected outcomes of the utilization stage are:

- Constant internal (if available), external, quality in use, and operational quality monitoring
- Quality baseline, updated with the results from the quality in use and operational quality monitoring
- Proactive detection of service level breaches and product failures
- Incident management, if applicable
- Request fulfillment, if applicable
- Corrective and preventive actions
- Utilization-inducted change requests fed to the support phase
- Continuous and effective system operation
- Achieved system owner/user satisfaction
- Quality records
- Quality-related retirement criteria.

2.2.3.2.5 Support Stage

During this stage, the system or software is deployed and operational, and logistics for operation and maintenance support should be already in place with the support and maintenance quality plan established in previous stages.

For any given change request of any type, the change management plan should also handle change requests coming from the quality engineering itself. Such change requests may be triggered by the observation of the results of quality in use measurement, for example. Quality-initiated changes within this phase should be the object of a complete impact analysis just like any other change request. If an organizational quality management system is in place, all these quality records should be kept.

In the maintenance quality plan, the business quality measures should be used as triggers to execute actions such as maintenance (perfective, adaptive, or preventive) to control software aging resulting from declining quality. Also, quality requirement changes are relatively probable during the support stage and that is why the quality engineer should have the decisional influence to propose and approve or reject these changes.

Finally, each time a change is accepted and implemented, the quality baseline should be reviewed using the results from the complete business quality V&V and quality implementation V&V. The processes for quality evaluation should be included in the support quality plan.

Once the change is released, the quality engineer should perform an evaluation of the updated system to make sure the stakeholders' quality requirements are still met.

All actions undertaken during this stage shall be governed by the established support and maintenance quality plan.

The quality engineer should be responsible for the management and implementation of change requests affecting quality attributes, and should propose required quality improvements and initiate them.

All approved and implemented changes to the system or software in this stage should trigger measurement and evaluation of the resulting quality attributes to ensure compliance with the quality requirements.

The expected outcomes of the support stage are:

- Quality engineer's active participation in change management
  - requesting changes
  - assessing impacts on system/product's quality
  - accepting/rejecting change requests
  - updating the quality baseline
  - reviewing releases' results
- Quality engineer's active participation in designing the change
- Quality engineer's active participation in quality implementation V&V
- Up-to-date quality baseline (attributes, requirements and selected measures, V&V data, quality in use data, etc.)
- Reduced risk of system premature aging
- Quality engineer's active participation in reviews
- Updated quality records.

2.2.3.2.6   Retirement Stage

The retirement stage is executed to retire the existing system or software and eventually transfer its services to a new one, while preserving data quality, integrity and security. ISO/IEC 2474-1 mentions the necessity of having the retirement enabling (support) system before the retirement process actually begins. In most software-intensive systems cases, the retirement enabling system will provide data conversion and archival services, so security is a prime quality concern to be engineered in the retirement enabling data archival system [55].

If data are to be kept, data quality must be managed so the retirement enabling data conversion system must be properly engineered, that is, with the proper quality engineering activities in order to preserve data integrity, suitability, and accuracy. Compliance with applicable legal or ethical constraints is also required, and has a broader scope than just privacy (e.g., escrow, records retention, grandfather clauses, public records access, etc.).

If the existing system or software is to be replaced, its latest baseline of quality attributes, quality requirements, and selected measures can be reused as an input for the definition of the future system or software.

The retirement stage should also serve as an opportunity to collect a rather unique set of data and lessons on quality throughout the system's lifespan. It seems profitable to integrate these data as a whole and feed them back to the organizational quality management system, if such a system exists. A final and global post-mortem review should also be performed if the existing system or software is to be replaced by a new one. The lessons learned will provide priceless insights for the future system development.

The retirement stage ensures a secure data disposal or archival is performed. If data are to be carried over to a new replacement system, the retirement stage will provide a data conversion system, which ensures that data quality and integrity are preserved.

The quality in use, external, and internal quality attributes, requirements, and selected measures baseline should be preserved for reuse in the replacement system's development; records and results can be integrated and synthesized as to provide feedback to the organizational quality management system, if such a system exists, and to the replacement system's lifecycle phases if such is planned.

The expected outcomes of the retirement phase are:

- Data with the proper quality, integrity, and security
- Reusable quality attributes, requirements, and selected measures
- Lessons learned on product and process quality.

2.2.4 Software Quality V&V

V&V, or verification and validation, represent the software quality engineering activities that correspond to system and user tests or, more popularly, to questions: whether the system was built *correctly* and whether the *correct* system was built.

Let's recall from the previous section: quality measurement should be:

- Properly designed as quality tests
- Executed in every stage where related artifacts are produced
- As unobtrusive as possible, which means embedded into main tests.

Although these three points are important, they do not cover all matter that makes quality V&V. Before being executed, V&V should be carefully planned as different quality attributes can be verified in different phases of the life cycle of a system or software. For example, static (internal) quality can be only verified during the coding phase, as in preceding phases there is no code yet, but in the following phases the code disappears into a running product. Going further in the same direction, the dynamic (external) quality requires a running code, so the first moment any measure may be taken is in the phase of system tests.

Now, when tests are designed and planned, their execution can take place, but that activity requires additional preparations in the form of choosing measurement techniques and tools and, of course, a proper form of documenting both tests and their results.

After the measures are taken and documented, the quality engineer has at his or her disposal data that in their raw form are completely meaningless. To turn them into usable information, he or she has to apply appropriate evaluation and interpretation mechanisms. This process was in part discussed in Sections 2.1.4 and 2.1.5 and will be continued in the next chapters.

The information obtained in the course of this process has value only if used, which means it has to be analyzed from the perspective of the impact associated with characteristics or behavior of the system or software it represents.

Finally, all the above effort would be booked on "loss" side in the project ledger if no managerial reaction followed.

2.2.4.1 *Designing, Planning, and Executing V&V*

A very good initial step of the design of software quality V&V would be to take ISO/IEC 25040 and ISO/IEC 25041 standards and, treating them as a quality evaluator's manual, identify what should be measured and when. ISO/IEC 25040 helps in this process, assisting the quality engineer further in defining the scope of the evaluation and developing an evaluation strategy.

Such an action would most probably achieve acceptable results, but would it be smart? Why should the quality engineer design from scratch something that has already been partially designed?

Section 2.2.2 discussed in detail the design of quality and in its conclusion presented a *personalized quality implementation map* with all the identified and required attributes and measures in place. This part already identifies *what* should be done.

The next step is to decide how to verify it, so a practical question would be: When should the design of tests begin?

The whole effort of identifying and defining quality requirements is the first place where tests design could commence, which in the case of quality requirements covers three consecutive phases of a system or software life cycle:

- Requirements identification and definition phase: quality in use and partially external/dynamic quality
- System or software design: external/dynamic and partially internal/static quality
- Program (or code) design: internal/static quality.

2.2.4.1.1   Example

In the requirements phase, one of the identified quality requirements was *enhanced user error protection* (external/dynamic quality, characteristic "usability"). This requirement, in practical terms, means that the developed system has to have exceptional control mechanisms over the user's interactions with it, such as control of data being input (limits, formats, etc.) or sequences of actions (such as "don't let the bomb go off before the missile is launched"). The design of a quality test for this subcharacteristic would begin with identifying all user interactions that invoke data input or sequences of actions. In the next step, for every of these interactions a "stupid" test scenario could be identified and designed. By "stupid" we mean a scenario that attempts to force incorrect, unprofessional, or simply a negligent user's behavior over the system. Now, to verify if the user error protection is really *exceptional* we would seek data on how many of these "stupid" scenarios succeeded (so the control mechanisms failed) and against how many of them the system effectively exhibited the necessary defense mechanisms.

If we combine this test design with the corresponding part of *personalized quality implementation map* we have almost everything required for effective quality V&V of this particular quality requirement:

- Test scenarios
- Quality attributes and corresponding measures
- Targeted values.

The same pattern could be applied to the requirements resulting in system design and program design phases, with perhaps a small modification applicable in program design phase. As was stated earlier, in the program (or code) design phase we face static (internal) quality characteristics of the developed system, so the idea of scenarios would not work well here since there will be no "action," just lines of code on a screen or a page of paper. So instead of using the idea of *test scenarios* we better apply the term of *test content*, where the conditions of the execution of a given test can be defined. For example, the high-level quality requirement of *enhanced maintainability* (external quality), after the whole process of decomposition, may end on the program design level in a form of *modification efficiency* attribute (*modifiability* subcharacteristic). This attribute has at least two facets:

- Evaluating time used for modifications against the quantity of these modifications, and/or
- Analyzing the conditions that would influence this efficiency, such as code complexity.

The test content could then state: the design of the program should allow for as many as possible modifications in as short as possible time. Well, imagine the face of the developer if you ask him or her to help you execute such a test.

The other option for this test could state: since the modification efficiency is closely linked to the complexity of the code architecture (design), it is required that the resulting code does not exceed the value X of the McCabe cyclomatic complexity metric [56]. And this test can be executed in an unobtrusive way, through applying static code analysis tools.

In the classical approach, the test phase is where the tests are designed, planned, and executed, but with the technique presented here the quality engineer arrives in this phase with the job at least partially done: the tests are identified and designed in terms of test scenarios/contents, measures, and targeted levels. What remains to be done still is to build for each test the *full test case*, which means at least supplying the following information (based on the evaluation process from ISO/IEC 25040):

- Test case ID (number, title)
- Originating quality requirement
- Test case purpose (quality attribute to be verified)
- Test case content or scenario
- Test execution procedures (these procedures should also take into account the feature of unobtrusiveness of the test)
- Test environment
- Test schedule and planning
- Test tools and technology
- Test targeted values
- Pass/fail criteria
- Documentation of test data and evaluation results
- Additional comments.

The next step, the V&V execution, has to follow the test plan developed earlier, the requirements and conditions defined in every test case, and, of course, the quality evaluation process, which, in case of this book, is the one proposed in ISO/IEC 25040 and ISO/IEC 25041.

From a practical perspective, the quality V&V execution mirrors quality design and quality test design processes and strictly follows the software quality life cycle model discussed in Section 2.1.4. The tests of static/internal quality can be executed only in the coding part of the production phase, the tests of dynamic/external quality can be executed in majority in the system tests phase and partially in user tests phase, and quality in use can only be tested in user test part.

2.2.4.2   *Impact Analysis and Managerial Decisions*

The execution of quality V&V produces data that are linked to identified quality requirements and desired quality attributes of the system or software. The analysis of these data has one, main purpose: identification of the impact associated with a quality characteristic or the behavior it represents on the developed system or software and the overall project.

Let's begin with the impact on the system or software. Independently of the phase where the tests were executed, the results may impact either only the phase directly or propagate further into the life cycle, invoking modifications in a domino effect. For example, if the modification efficiency discussed in the previous section, evaluated indirectly through the McCabe metric, shows that the resulting code is too complex to be easily modified, so in consequence maintained, the impact is local to the phase and can be remedied through the program redesign/recoding/retesting effort. But what will be the impact if this small deficiency is *not* remedied? In the worst case scenario, weeks, months or even years after the system is put into utilization, the costs of ongoing maintenance may suddenly spike up or, when worse comes to worst, the whole operation of the organization may be put on hold because required modification is too difficult and time-consuming to be executed painlessly.

Further down the same line, if the previously discussed user error protection proves inadequate during the external/dynamic quality tests, the impact will propagate back to the coding phase, and eventually, depending on the severity of the deficiency, to the design phase where all the against-user-error defense mechanisms were conceived. So the correction may require partial redesign in one phase of the life cycle, recoding in the other, and a new set of (usually regression) tests in all phases that led to the manifestation of the inefficient user error protection. The impact of letting this deficiency go uncorrected may vary from a strange date on the letter to a friend to an explosion in a nuclear plant, and has to be analyzed rather carefully (for the analysis of this perspective, refer to Section 1.2.2).

When the system or software finally gets to the phase of user tests, mostly quality in use is verified and the impact of the deficiencies on this level is the biggest in practically every direction. If the new system or software has been ordered to remedy the decreasing effectiveness (accuracy and completeness with which users achieve specified goals) of the organization's staff and quality in use tests demonstrate that this effectiveness is unsatisfactory, the impact may go back even to the quality requirements definition level. For example, in the case where, technologically speaking, the required increase of effectiveness is undoable (the best available technology is not able to run "fast enough"), this requirement may require renegotiating. If the modification is possible, the reasons for effectiveness deficiency may be hidden in the design (designed processes, data analysis algorithms, database design, etc.), in technological choices (programming languages, operation systems, etc.) or even in bad coding or inefficient utilization of resources such as RAM or processors, so in the worst case scenario the whole life cycle may need to be partially executed again, including retesting the effectiveness at the end. The impact of not correcting an unsatisfactory level of effectiveness may end in a full-blown lose-lose scenario, where the customer (user) loses credibility and his or her customer base because the services (products) are not as satisfactory as the ones of his or her competition, and the developer's organization loses the customer, image, and position on the market as unable to deliver the system or software of required, agreed, and paid for quality. The simple process model helping this part of impact analysis is presented in Fig. 2.39.

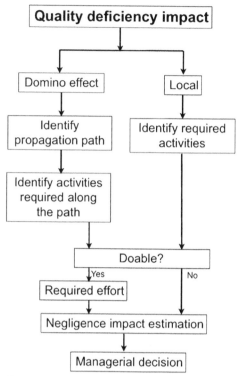

Figure 2.39   System or software quality deficiency impact analysis process.

In the context of the overall project, nothing that happens is without consequences. Every negative result of quality V&V should (ideally) be reacted to and as such should make the quality-related part of managerial process where the appropriate decisions would be made. A simple way of illustrating this part of the process would be to look at it from the perspective of the project financial landscape.

From a managerial and financial point of view, any quality deficiency in the developed system or software can be defined by the following parameters:

- Severity
- Cost of correction
- Cost of negligence.

When the quality V&V results indicate quality deficiencies, with the exception of internal quality corrections, nothing usually happens before getting the managerial "go–no go" because, in case of "go," money, time and resources must follow. What makes a "go" part? The costs of negligence exceeding the costs of corrections and/ or high severity of the deficiency. What makes a "no go" part? The costs of corrections exceeding the costs of negligence and low or medium severity of the deficiency.

If we look at this somehow simplistic way of making important managerial decisions, we will probably suspect that it must be a rather popular technique, considering the quality of our contemporary IT products.

There is another important, managerial process-related aspect of quality V&V: the detection of systemic errors in the overall quality engineering approach. The continuous monitoring of quality V&V results and related impacts should, after some time, help discover systemic reasons for recurring problems in achieving the required quality in realized projects.

The recurrence of difficulties in engineering quality into the developed system or software should, depending on their nature, trigger the revision of at least:

- The existing quality engineering expertise

- Human resources involved in quality engineering

- Basic quality engineering framework used in projects (quality models, measures)

- Measurement and evaluation methods and processes

- Tools and technologies used in the quality engineering process

- Documentation of V&V passed, expertise accumulation, and usage of lessons learned.

2.2.5   Additional Aspects of Software Quality Engineering

As was discussed in Section 2.1, obtaining the quality of a software product or system is an engineering effort, quite similar in its form and objectives to that of developing a product or system, and as such should have adequate ramifications, resources, processes, models, and practices. From this perspective, the overall project can have two strongly interlinked processes (development and quality engineering) aiming at the same final objective, but sometimes operating on bases that can invoke "conflicts of interests," be it process-related, technical, technological, or budgetary (see Section 1.2.1). Section 2.2.5.1 analyzes conflicts that can appear within the basic change control process of a software project.

The strong relation between these processes invokes the subject of traceability, but not only from the developed artifact to its originating functional requirement or from a quality engineering to-do to its related quality requirement, but also the cross-traceability that would link both processes into one harmonious structure, where the existence of every project artifact can be justified by a complete path to its originating functional requirement and to related quality requirements. This subject is discussed in Section 2.2.5.2.

2.2.5.1   *Conflict Identification and Resolution*
Apart from the common duties of planning and managing a project, managing software quality engineering also requires a considerably difficult duty of change and

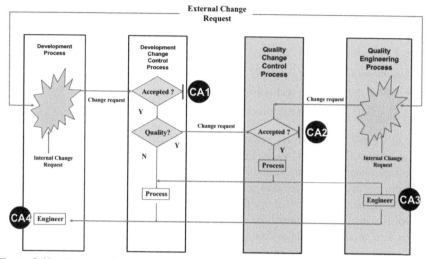

Figure 2.40   Change and conflict management in software quality engineering.

conflict management. The higher-than-usual level of difficulty of this task comes from heavy interdependence between development and quality engineering processes and their final results.

The diagram from Fig. 2.40 shows possible interactions and branching combinations when a change request comes. If a change request is originated on the "functional" (be it internal, from within the project, or external, from the customer) side of the process, it does not rule out the impact on quality. On the contrary, an experienced quality engineer would rather suspect that such an impact exists and try to verify and validate it. If this is the case, the same verification, validation, feasibility, and (cross) impact analysis would have to be applied in both "functional" and "quality" aspects. In case of a change request originating on the "quality" side of the process, the software development engineer would have to be involved in evaluating the feasibility and impact of the required change, as most quality aspects are demonstrated through the behavior of the code. In other words, any change request will most probably impact both functional and quality aspects of the developed system or software and they will have to be dealt with keeping in mind the overall best possible result.

In this complex task, finding and solving conflicts is as natural as breathing. It is rather obvious that these conflicts may emerge from any place within such a complicated process so the following few examples are given only in an attempt to illustrate the gravity of the problem (CA1 to CA4 refer to conflict points of origin in Fig. 2.40):

- CA1—between functional and quality requirements
- CA2—between existing and new quality requirements
- CA3—on the level of the design of quality

- CA4—different conflicts related to technical aspects of implementation
- Conflicts related to business domain
- Conflicts related to budget
- Conflicts related to schedule
- Conflicts related to technology
- Conflicts related to resources.

Let's briefly examine an example: a conflict between *functional and quality requirements* (CA1 and CA4 in Fig. 2.40). Imagine the user's new functionality request coming somewhere in the middle of the project. The project is in motion, requirements are known, the design is relatively stable, the balance between quality and development efforts is set up, the budget is distributed. If the new requirement is basically doable, the immediate concern is its eventual impact on quality, which means how much more engineering effort will be required to accompany the new functionality with at least minimal, acceptable quality, and is this new quality requirement feasible? The first part of the conflict is usually rooted in *resources* and *budget*. If resources are limited and budget is "inflexible," the new functionality to be realized will have to "steal" part of both from somewhere else, so either one of existing developed functionalities will suffer (unlikely) or quality budget will be shortened, so some part of the engineering effort will be put on hold. And here you have a conflict.

The second part is related rather to *technological* consequences impacting quality engineering within the given project. Imagine a quality requirement of high *maintainability* of the developed system. This requirement translates mostly into "all elegant, clear, low coupling, high cohesion, no shortcuts" type of system or software realization. In the case of older database systems the high maintainability would be paid by lower speed, so when the request coming from the customer is a faster database, the maintainability will be first to suffer. And here there is a conflict.

Now let's play this card in the opposite direction. A customer's requirement that comes in the middle of the project is the *enhanced maintainability*. The customer's reasons for such a requirement may be to reduce future exploitation costs by maintaining the system him- or herself or installing one of the system instances in the country where the supplier has no presence. The potential echo on the development side of the project may be immense, impacting design, coding, testing, documentation, and training and as such may be deemed unfeasible or too expensive for the customer to accept it.

Every change request, independently of its nature and originator (the development team or the customer), if accepted, will influence the overall schedule of the project, quality engineering included. The schedule adjustments that would be acceptable for the development side of the project may not be equally comfortable for quality side, so this will require some kind of internal negotiation, and if the results influence the overall project schedule, it may require negotiations with the customer.

Last but not least, a professional concern of the quality engineer is the tools that might support change and conflict management process. The existing change control and configuration management tools are mostly focused on functional and nonfunctional aspects of the developed system or software and as such address in a limited way the need for controlling the cross-dependences between development and quality engineering. However, since these tools usually use a database of some type as the system's foundation, it should be possible to modify both record structures and queries to better reflect the development–quality engineering dependence. The following section presents the models that can be useful in introducing the required modifications in these tools.

2.2.5.2   *Traceability in Software Quality Engineering*

Let's recall the already mentioned important business and software engineering rule: any software or system component that cannot be traced to at least one requirement has been developed for nothing and the resources used to develop it must be booked as a loss.

In the case of linking software quality engineering and development into one, coherent traceability mechanism, the approach presented in Fig. 2.41 would help. It shows in a simplified form the general idea of identifying any artifact within a project by describing its traceability links.

The diagram in Fig. 2.41 could be read as follows: the development artifact A is originated by a functional requirement B that is associated with quality requirement C that is translated into quality engineering "to-do" D that is applied to development artifact A. In a correct traceability situation this phrase should be readable forward and backward (just try it, for fun). If you find yourself in a situation where this phrase goes in only one way (missing arrow or arrowhead), something is wrong with the artifact you are observing.

The classic traceability approach, presented in its modified form in Fig. 2.42, documents the links between generic phases of the development process and their related by-products to requirements. These links must exist all in order to create a functionally valid software product.

Applying at the same time the software quality implementation model SQIM (Section 2.3.1), ISO/IEC 9126, ISO/IEC 25000, and the Consolidated Quality Life Cycle (CQL) model (Section 2.3.5) allowed for creating a complementary model

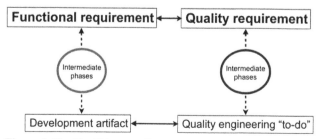

Figure 2.41   Identifying an artifact within a project by describing its traceability links.

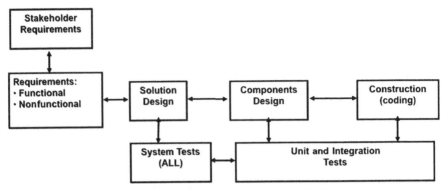

Figure 2.42   Modified traceability model for development process (DTM).

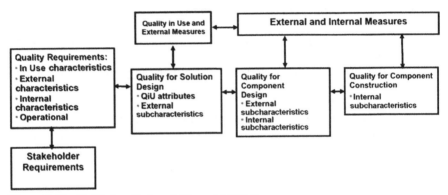

Figure 2.43   Modified quality traceability model (QTM).

dedicated to quality traceability, where every link from the lowest level quality measure could be traced to quality requirements (Fig. 2.43).

Merging the two models and adding an intermediate influence layer between the two parts gives a consolidated traceability model (CTM) allowing for building a complete functionality/quality traceability matrix (Fig. 2.44).

The model incorporates both technological and procedural structures helping to identify the correspondence between the stage of development, related by-products, associated quality elements (by-products or attributes), and requirements of all types. For example, the phase of solution (system) design is associated with corresponding system tests on the "development" side and with design of quality for the overall system (so quality in use and partially external quality) and corresponding quality measures on the "quality" side. The engineer can thus monitor the relationships among all of them and then trace them back to their relevant requirements.

Finally, applying CTM in the conflict resolution process discussed in the previous section helps in both identifying and choosing applicable technical/engineering solutions, and in analyzing eventual impacts of the conflict.

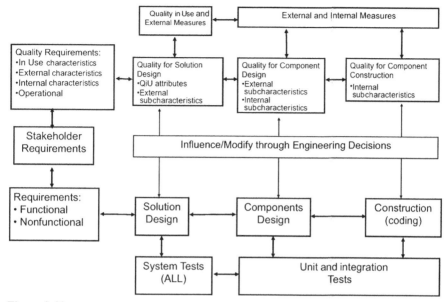

Figure 2.44   Consolidated traceability model for software quality engineering.

2.3   PRACTICAL CONSIDERATIONS

Everything what was discussed in previous sections had in the background a recurring idea that quality engineering is a process similar to the one applied in development and as such should have similar methodologies and tools, and should follow a similar process model. Yes, but *which model?*

2.3.1   Software Quality Implementation Process Model SQIM

The definition of software quality engineering presented in Section 2.1.1 of this chapter states: "The application of a continuous, systematic, disciplined, quantifiable approach to the development and maintenance of quality throughout the whole life cycle of software products and systems; that is, the application of quality engineering to software." In more practical terms, it indicates that quality to be attained cannot be "made" here and there, a little bit today and some more tomorrow. In the matter of fact, a good, recommended practice is to start engineering the quality at the same second the development project is opened. This approach requires, however, a tool, a method that will rule and control quality engineering activities in concert with these of software development. Such a tool, called Software Quality Implementation Model (SQIM), is presented in Fig. 2.45. The four basic hypotheses laid at foundations of developing SQIM are:

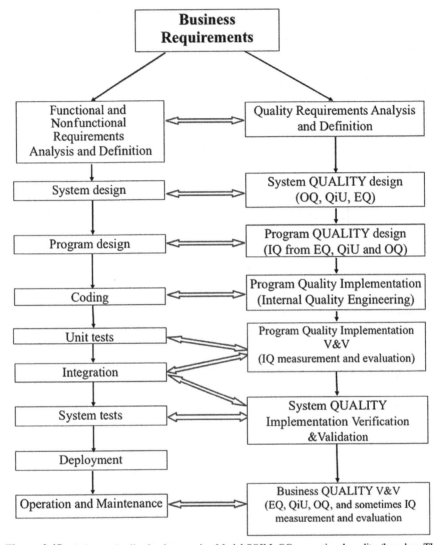

Figure 2.45   Software Quality Implementation Model SQIM. OQ: operational quality (based on TL 9000); QiU: quality in use (from ISO/IEC 9126 and ISO/IEC 25010); EQ: External quality (from ISO/ IEC 9126 and ISO/IEC 25010); IQ: internal quality (from ISO/IEC 9126 and ISO/IEC 25010).

1. Engineering of quality into a software product is an effort that should be conducted throughout the whole life cycle of software.

2. The process of quality engineering is in many points similar to a development process, and it seems appropriate that it follows similar rules and applies similar structures.

3. Since there exist several software development process models, SQIM is based on most widely recognized and accepted one, the generic model pub-

lished in ISO/IEC 15288 – Information Technology – Life Cycle Management – System Life Cycle Processes [25].

4. The quality model that SQIM adheres to is the one that is widely accepted and recognized, the quality model from ISO/IEC 9126 and ISO/IEC 25010.

SQIM is organized in phases that correspond to phases of the generic development process with indicated activities that are required from a software quality engineer in order to attain quality in each of the phases. It can be noted that the subject of complexity of software quality requirement definition is clearly addressed in SQIM, offering to the reader guidance in what and when could and should be identified and defined.

Further down, the model indicates engineering activities that should be implemented in consecutive phases of development process in order to comply with defined quality requirements.

Each phase of SQIM has its own set of activities and subprocesses that were discussed in previous sections; however, a few clarifications of the correspondence between SQIM and ISO/IEC 15288 life cycle model may help better execute the quality implementation.

While requirement definition, analysis, and architectural (system) design phases are basically the same in both models, SQIM additionally mentions the program design phase and breaks down the implementation process from ISO/IEC 15288 into coding and unitary tests. The objective of this differentiation is to allow for more precise internal/static quality implementation and verification. In the program design phase, the quality engineering "to-dos" are integrated into the overall code architecture, in the coding phase they are realized, and in the unit test phase they are verified as the part of unitary testing process. Another comment is required concerning the phase of system tests and corresponding system quality implementation V&V. Depending on the source, the phase of system tests either contains functional and nonfunctional tests only, and then passes to transition and user tests phase (as it is in ISO/15288, where verification phase leads to transition and validation), or it contains user acceptance tests as well. In practice, the latter are sometimes done in the third way, in two separate parts: part one, in a simulated user environment installed in the developer's premises where the representatives of the end user execute the preliminary user test suite, and part two, when full acceptance tests are run in a real operation environment after the transition (installation) of the system.

In SQIM, to more easily manage all these options, the system tests phase covers all three categories of tests. Such compression in no way changes the required quality engineering activities, as the basic difference between the sequences proposed in ISO/IEC 15288 and SQIM is place of their execution. Quality in use tests that have to be executed by the user in the validation phase of ISO/IEC 15288 are exactly the same from the design and execution perspective if put in the "bigger" system test phase of SQIM.

Having in mind the fact that in the industry life runs fast and engineers do not always have time for profound studies, the "reader's digest" version of SQIM has been developed in form of the Consolidated Quality Life Cycle (CQL) model is presented further in Section 2.3.5.

2.3.2 Software Quality Engineering Resources

Who within the organization that develops software or system should be responsible for engineering quality into a final product? Should it be the architect, the developer, the tester, or perhaps the project manager? Should an organization have a specialized quality engineering group, or only one person, or maybe just a specialist who in the morning wears a "quality hat" and in the afternoon a "test hat"? Should he or she be a free electron who bothers "seriously working people" with unreal quality ideas and demands, or be a full-blooded member of a development team? We will seek the answer analyzing software quality implementation model SQIM from the previous section.

If we go through the left-hand side of the model, we see the classic passage from phase to phase with dedicated specialists in each of them, thus we have architects, developers, testers, and so on. We know that the developer is better in coding than the architect and that the latter may have some problems when put into a hands-on testing team. So they are specialists in their domains, because we want them to do best what they were hired to do.

If we go through the right-hand side of SQIM, we see a sequence of phases where one specialist or a group of specialists in the same domain pass from one phase to the next as the project advances, and the knowledge of this domain does not always adhere well to the domains present in the left-hand side of the model. So, to sum up, in a small or medium-size project, the left-hand side would require three different specialists to be correctly executed, while right-hand side would require only one, but with considerably different expertise. Let's name again this expertise:

- Working knowledge of quality engineering framework (quality models and measures)
- Expertise in identifying and defining all quality requirements, those stated, implied, and of which the customer is unaware
- Ability to translate requirements into attributes and measures,
- Ability to transform required attributes into engineering "to-dos" comprehensible and executable by technical specialists
- Expertise in quality evaluation planning and design
- Expertise in designing, planning, and executing the quality tests
- Expertise in analyzing test results and drawing correct, quality engineering-sound, and applicable conclusions
- Rather advanced negotiation skills.

If we add to this list the observation that some of the quality engineer's duties may be considered "annoying" by the specialists from left-hand side of the model, mixing the left- and right-hand sides' responsibilities would probably lead to unrequired results. Besides being (in a fashion) the creator of quality of the developed system or software, the quality engineer is also its watchdog, and this requires sometimes saying "no" to people who do not always see it as saving their skin. Sometimes saying "sorry, the quality of this artifact is inadequate" may be met with an unfriendly reaction that would create a conflict of interest if the same person did both development and the critiques.

It seems rather obvious, then, that a quality engineer position should be given to a quality engineer, trained and educated in this particular domain. Whether it should be one or more specialists strictly depends on the size and complexity of the project, but *none* should not be an option, unless one wishes to produce more blue-screen-quality systems.

2.3.3 Synchronizing Software Quality Engineering with the Software Development Process

The subject of synchronization quality engineering with development activities attempts to address the practical question of how to do it. On a more practical note, should quality engineering-related activities be inscribed into continuous development effort or rather be regular but discrete interventions?

There is no one, good answer to all these questions. A large, mature, and professional organization would most probably steer in direction of a specialized group, with members being continuously involved in works of development teams, while a startup could be more tempted by discrete solution with a part-time quality specialist. This all depends on the available resources and goals to be reached.

Whatever the decision, the person making it will have to take into consideration the pros and cons of both discrete and continuous synchronization methods and leverage them against the particular situation. When comparing both methods the first impression may be that the discrete approach (e.g., Fig. 2.46) is rarely recommendable. If the developed software is created for the first time (so has some R&D taste) this impression has its merit, but when system is being continuously manufactured and sold for several years, most probably all the "secrets" are known by heart by the development team and quality engineering may be quite effective even if applied in form presented in Fig. 2.46.

Continuous synchronization between quality engineering and software development processes (Fig. 2.47), while being much more resource consuming, offers at the same time an incomparably higher level of controllability and effectiveness.

The role of a software quality engineer in a continuous process is that of a specialist who has to do his or her own work (quality-related engineering) before acting as a member of a development team. In some phases of the project, this role requires very active and sometimes aggressive participation (as in all design and some test phases), while in some others it is reduced to assisting the developers or supporting the testers (as in the coding phase).

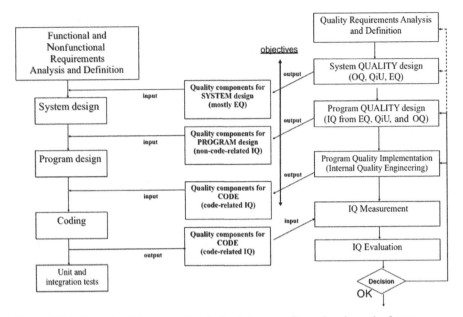

Figure 2.46   Example of discrete synchronization between quality engineering and software.

Whatever the phase of the project, the quality engineer brings unique expertise to the team, allowing the "nonquality" specialists develop software able to demonstrate high quality and helping to maintain the budget and schedule.

2.3.4 Appling SQIM to Some Popular Life Cycle Models

The following four diagrams attempt to help the potential user of SQIM to map this model to a development process of the most popular choice.

In the case of the V-model, the mapping to SQIM is straightforward (Fig. 2.48), as the V-model itself is very closely linked to the model proposed in ISO/IEC 15288. Mapping SQIM to the basic spiral model requires some repositioning of SQIM phases in order to build the applicative links (Fig. 2.49). As the third quadrant ("Develop, verify next-level product") concentrates most of the engineering activities, corresponding phases of SQIM have to be concentrated accordingly.

In the prototyping model the application of SQIM requires only taking into consideration the repetitive nature of each phase of this model. Each phase of SQIM associated with its counterpart in prototyping model will have to run through the same loops of verifying and validating before the obtained status will allow for moving to the next phase (Fig. 2.50). While it may appear tiring, running the quality engineering through all the "prototyping loops" may create excellent final results.

Last but not least, mapping SQIM to the incremental model can be reduced to the choice from the three options previously discussed. The very nature of the incremental model (Fig. 2.51) describes more the way in which a software product is

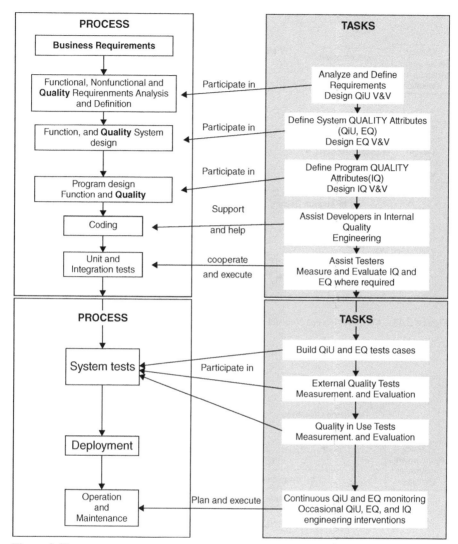

Figure 2.47   Continuous synchronization between quality engineering and software.

being *delivered* than the way in which it is really developed. In other words, every increment within the model may follow a different development process (like any one from the three discussed here), still fully adhering to the definition of the increment.

2.3.5   Consolidated Quality Life Cycle Model

The Consolidated Quality Life Cycle (CQL) model was created to help a software quality engineer quickly identify and apply required normative and/or scientific

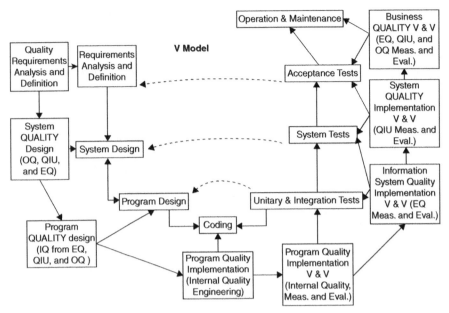

Figure 2.48   Mapping between V-model and SQIM.

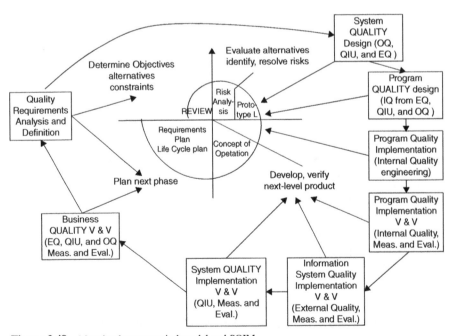

Figure 2.49   Mapping between spiral model and SQIM.

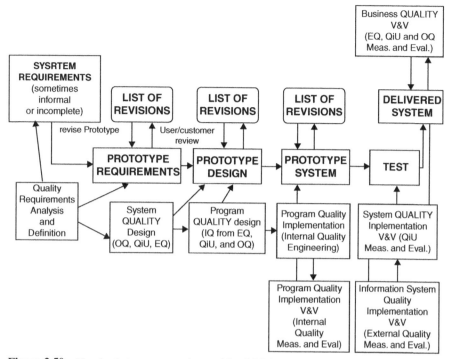

Figure 2.50   Mapping between prototyping model and SQIM.

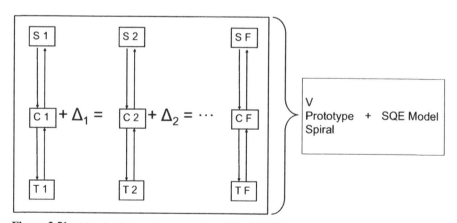

Figure 2.51   Mapping between incremental model and SQIM.

support depending on the phase of a system life cycle in which the project actually is. As the result, the software quality engineer may be able to identify and define quality requirements and then, using the recommended references, identify measures that serve best the purposes of the project. As helpful as it may be, the model still bears all the characteristics of a menu, which implies that the correctness of the decisions based on this menu depends on the user and the level of his or her professional knowledge.

ISO 9001		
Common TL 9000 Requirements		
Hardware Specific Requirements	Software Specific Requirements	Service Specific Requirements
Common TL 9000 Metrics		
Hardware Metrics	Software Metrics	Service Metrics

Figure 2.52   Basic TL9000 model (adapted from [37]).

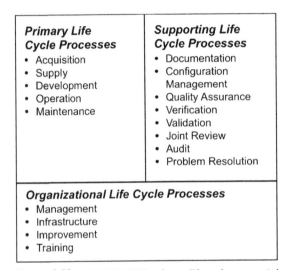

Figure 2.53   ISO/IEC 12207 software life cycle process (adapted from [57]).

As can easily be found, the major contribution to the CQL model comes from the ISO/IEC 9126, ISO/IEC 14598, and ISO/IEC TL9000 standards (Fig. 2.52). All of those standards have been available for several years, with some of them being adopted as national standards (ISO/IEC 9126 was adopted as the national standard in Japan), which guarantees the appropriate base for the application and normative support for CQL model. As both ISO/IEC 9126 and ISO/IEC 14598 are being gradually replaced by ISO/IEC 25000 SQuaRE series of standards, the CQL model also evolves to keep its applicative value intact.

Due to the nature of the CQL model and its broad applicability, it was decided to also consider other standards for their additional contribution. The ISO/IEC 15288:2007—System and Software Engineering—System Lifecycle Processes (Fig. 2.53) [25] and ISO/IEC 12207:2008—Information Technology—Software Lifecycle Processes (Fig. 2.54) [57] were found to be important contributors to the final version of CQL model. In both cases it was found crucial for CQL model to adhere to these standards, as they represent the most recognized and stable modeling of the generic

Enterprise Processes	Project Processes
• Enterprise Management Process • Investment Management Process • System Life Cycle Management Process • Resource Management Process	• Planning Process • Assessment Process • Control Process • Decision Making Process • Risk Management Process • Configuration Management Process
	Technical Processes
	• Stakeholders Needs Definition Process • Requirements Analysis Process • Architectural Design Process • Implementation Process • Integration Process • Verification Process
Agreement Processes	• Transition Process
• Acquisition Process • Supply Process	• Validation Process • Operation and Maintenance Process • Disposal Process

Figure 2.54   ISO/IEC 15288 system life cycle process (adapted from [25]).

processes within software engineering domain. One of the additional important arguments for applying the ISO/IEC 12207 and ISO/IEC 15288 models in CQL model is the harmonization project being conducted within ISO/IEC JTC1 SC7, having as the objective to align, synchronize, and modernize both standards so they reflect the latest developments in the area of software engineering.

Finally, the following references were also considered as contributors to CQL:

- ISO/IEC 15939, Software Engineering—Software Measurement Process [21]
- Project Management Book of Knowledge [58]
- ISO 10006, Quality Management—Guidelines to Quality in Project Management [59]
- Guide to the Software Engineering Body of Knowledge SWEBOK [34]
- Architecture Tradeoff Analysis Initiative [60].

These positions represent important references to CQL model auxiliary areas such as software measurement processes (helpful in quality measurement and evaluation) or project management.

The analysis conducted after the development of the first version of CQL indicated that the model contained phases with little or no quality engineering standards support. Figure 2.55 shows phases where normative support is nonexistent ("Transition" and "Integration") and phases that are poor in terms of quality engineering standards that could be securely applied ("Architectural Design").

The next version of CQL model with the proposed additions resulting from the aforementioned observations is presented in Fig. 2.56.

In the course of the development of the CQL model it has also been found that while for the professionals, the CQL model is relatively simple and easy to follow, for novices it may still remain difficult. In order to further support and simplify the work of industry specialists responsible for software quality engineering, a CQL-ISO/

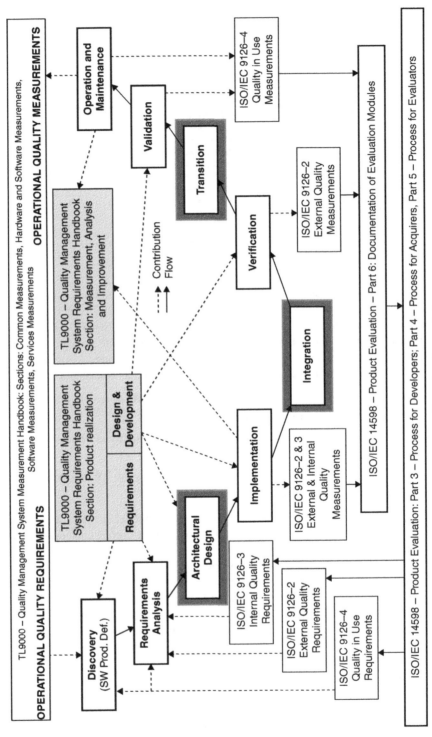

Figure 2.55 Phases of CQL model with poor or no support from quality engineering standards.

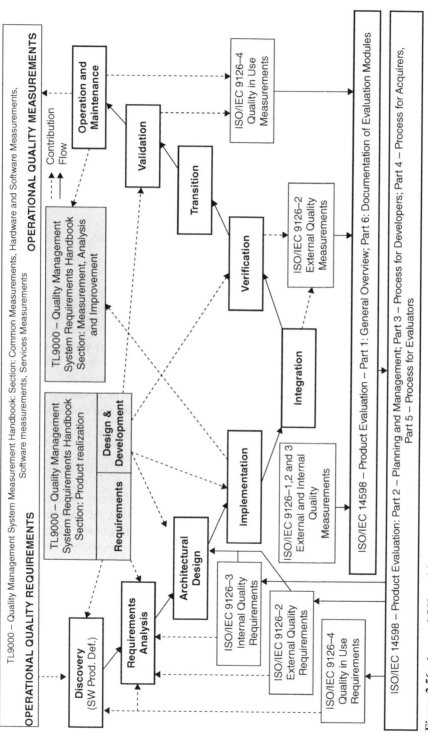

Figure 2.56 Improved CQL model.

129

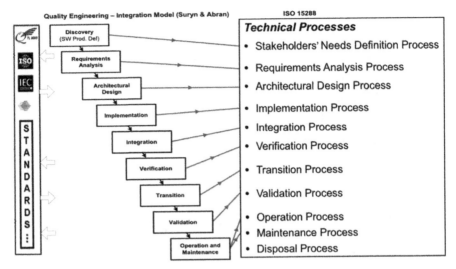

Figure 2.57   CQL-ISO/IEC 15288 mapping model.

IEC 15288 mapping model has been created. The mapping model shown in Fig. 2.57 allows for easier referencing of development models and their related technical processes to these applied in CQL model. The proposed CQL model will be discussed with the assumption that the software product does not exist yet.

Discovery Phase. This phase places the whole process on a business environment level, where three sets of requirements have to be identified and defined:

- Functional and nonfunctional requirements of the product
- Operational quality requirements, if applicable
- Quality in use requirements.

It is important to note here that according to the model of quality in software life cycle defined in ISO/IEC 9126-1 and later in ISO/IEC 25010, the requirements of quality in use contribute to specifying external quality requirements, which in turn contribute to specifying internal quality requirements. This subprocess clearly indicates that the attributes of quality in use have the direct impact on technical and technological decisions that (will) have to be taken when the development process starts. Continuing, the person responsible for defining new software product quality attributes will have to analyze quality in use characteristics, identify applicable measures, and assign target values for each of them. The ISO standards helpful when completing this task are ISO/IEC 9126-4 quality in use metrics and ISO/IEC 25022, when published.

It is also strongly recommended to refer in this and all consecutive phases of CQL to ISO/IEC 9126-1 or ISO/IEC 25010 quality model to keep continuous reference between detailed measures and attributes, and their originating characteristics and subcharacteristics.

Quality in use requirements help define success criteria of the new software product; however, alone, they may not be sufficient to assure the product's long-term success in the market. If the developed software product is of the OTS category, so dedicated to a massive user, such a success may be achieved when quality in use comes together with, among others, fulfilled operational quality requirements. The person responsible for defining new software product quality attributes will have to analyze operational quality requirements, identify applicable measures, and assign target values for each of them.

TL9000 Measurement Handbook [37] identifies four categories of requirements and/or measurements applicable to massive-sale software products:

- Common measurements: referring to number of problems reported, response time, overdue problem responsiveness, and on-time delivery
- Hardware and software measurements: referring to system outage
- Software measurements: referring to software installation and maintenance
- Service measurement: referring to service quality.

The final set of quality requirements obtainable in this phase and their targeted values, comprising of both operational quality and quality in use requirements, will then become the major milestone and contributor in the definition of functional and nonfunctional requirements of the future software product.

Requirements Analysis Phase. As this phase produces the translation of requirements (both quality and functional) from stakeholders' perspective into technical and technological terms, the level of abstraction changes from "business" to "system" and the environment changes to a system environment. In this environment the applicable quality requirements define external and internal quality attributes of software product.

The ISO standards helpful in this phase are:

- ISO/IEC 9126-2 external quality metrics
- ISO/IEC 9126-3 internal quality metrics
- ISO/IEC 25023 product quality measures, when published.

It has to be stressed here that the attributes of both external and internal quality being defined in this phase are direct descendants of quality requirements previously set up in the discovery phase, so the rule of traceability in software engineering is being conserved.

Architectural Design. System and program design make the usual content of this phase. As was discussed in Section 2.3.1 (SQIM), the quality design both on system and program level should accompany the design of the system itself. The results of this design should take form of engineering "to-dos" and be incorporated into the overall design effort. From this perspective, the existing standardization instruments offer a considerably usable, even if indirect, support. The ISO standards helpful in this phase are:

- ISO/IEC 9126-2 external quality metrics
- ISO/IEC 9126-3 internal quality metrics
- ISO/IEC 25023 product quality measures, when published.

Also, to facilitate the creation of the *personalized quality implementation map* it is recommended to use one of the available ISO quality model documents in order to eliminate quality characteristics not required for the developed system (or software).

Implementation Phase. Software coding and unit and integration testing make the usual contents of this phase. From a software quality engineering perspective, the last adjustments to internal quality requirements take place in this phase too. As the first in the whole life cycle, the implementation phase creates *a product* that can be measured and evaluated. It is true that the created product is intermediate and changes many times before becoming a ready-to-use solution, but due to this fact it is critical to measure and evaluate its quality. The product is now in a development environment and every iteration with measured and evaluated quality produces indications yielding further improvements. This process is very well addressed by appropriate standardization instruments that support measurement, documentation and evaluation of internal quality (and, if needed, external quality). The recommended procedure consists of:

- Measurements of internal and external quality attributes. Applicable documents are ISO/IEC 9126-2 and -3 and ISO/IEC 25023, when published.
- Documentation of measurements. Applicable documents are ISO/IEC 14598-6 documentation of evaluation modules or ISO/IEC 25042, when published.
- Evaluation of the quality of the intermediate products. Documents to be used, depending on the position of the evaluating entity, include ISO/IEC 14598-3 process for developers, 14598-4 process for acquirers or 14598-5 process for evaluators or ISO/IEC 25041.

The results of measurements of internal and external quality attributes are compared with target values assigned to them in previous phases and the conclusions are presented to development teams as the corrective measures of improvement.

The **Integration Phase** due to its nature may invoke quality interventions either on an internal/static or an external/dynamic level. During the phase itself the role of the quality engineer is rather limited, however, the outcomes of the phase may require his or her active involvement. A not-working integration may have sources principally in code or in higher-level design, which means that quality engineer may have to look back into what was wrongly done in both preceding phases, so the standardization support valid for these phases is also valid for the integration phase.

The **Verification Phase** makes a perfect opportunity for evaluation of the ready-to-use product quality in its system environment. In other words, the product is integrated (supposedly *complete*) and should correspond to stakeholder's functional and nonfunctional requirements. This explicitly means that external quality requirements have to be satisfied in this phase. The process of the evaluation of external quality requires a similar procedure as internal quality evaluation and is being similarly well supported by standardization instruments. The recommended procedure consists of:

- Measurements of external quality attributes. Applicable documents are ISO/IEC 9126-2 and ISO/IEC 25023, when published.
- Documentation of measurements. Applicable documents are ISO/IEC 14598–6 documentation of evaluation modules or ISO/IEC 25042, when published.

The results of measurements of external quality attributes are compared with target values assigned to them in previous phases. The resulting conclusions are presented to the development team as the corrective measures of improvement. The feedback may be deployed to different phases of the process depending on the level of the severity of discrepancies between required and obtained external quality.

The **Transition Phase** is a conveyor that transports the system or software from the developer site to the customer's operation environment. The phase itself can be as trivial as taking a CD and installing the software on a PC or may require several months of careful preparations before the actual system is up and running. From this perspective it is rather difficult to identify precise activities that may be required from a quality engineer, however, some quality parameters could be considered common for most forms of the transition phase. The *installability* (degree of effectiveness and efficiency with which a product or system can be successfully installed and/or uninstalled in a specified environment) and *coexistence* (degree to which a product can perform its required functions efficiently while sharing a common environment and resources with other products, without detrimental impact on any other product) will probably be the most frequent concerns of a quality engineer in the transition phase. Consequently, the required standardization support will be ISO/IEC 9126-2 external quality or ISO/IEC 25023, when published.

The **Validation Phase** moves the software product back to the business level, that is, to a business environment where satisfying the *business requirements* is the most important and ultimate task of the product. The system returns to its "black box" status (as it started in discovery phase) where the user validates its usefulness for conducting his or her business, usually with no regard to technicalities.

This again explicitly means that quality in use requirements have to be satisfied "here and now." The process of the evaluation of quality in use requires the same procedure as external quality evaluation and is being equally well supported by standardization instruments. The recommended procedure consists of:

- Measurements of quality in use attributes. Applicable documents are ISO/IEC 9126-4 and ISO/IEC 25022, when published.
- Documentation of measurements. Applicable documents are ISO/IEC 14598–6 documentation of evaluation modules or ISO/IEC 25042, when published.

The results of measurements of quality in use attributes are compared with target values assigned to them in previous phases. The resulting conclusions are presented to development team as the corrective measures of improvement. The feedback may be deployed to different phases of the process depending on the level of the severity of discrepancies between required and obtained quality in use.

The **Operation and Maintenance Phase** is recognized theoretically as the consecutive phase in the development process, while in fact this phase is defined by its own rules. The most important aspects distinguishing the operation and maintenance phase from all the previous phases are *time* and *control level*. The duration of operation and maintenance cannot be planned (even if there are attempts to forecast this period) and the phase itself is to a great extent driven by events. Last but not least is the environment, a business environment that practically excludes any long-term *active* experiments or measurements. But *passive* measurements are exactly what is needed in this phase.

Operational quality measurements, if applicable, require data, which to be representative have to be collected over relatively long period of time. In this case the procedure uses the TL9000 Quality Management System Measurements Handbook [38] in order to perform needed calculations and evaluate obtained operational quality. Depending on the area of measurement and evaluation, the results can be used immediately, for example, for improvements of the service quality, or in the next round of product development, if the evaluation indicates weaknesses of the product being in the field.

Applying measurements and evaluation of quality in use in the operation and maintenance phase proves its very sense especially in cases of large and complicated software products. The validation phase, where quality in use is being measured and evaluated for the first time, takes place in a relatively short period of time with limited exploration opportunities (e.g., a limited number of users), while the operation and maintenance phase offers natural circumstances with unlimited time and exhaustive conditions of exploitation.

2.3.5.1   *Applicability Considerations*

The discussion of the cycle of identification, definition, measurement, and evaluation of software product quality presented by the CQL model assumes the reader's familiarity with basic concepts used in ISO/IEC 14598 and ISO/IEC 9126 series. However, in the case of lack of such familiarity, the user of the CQL model can remedy it by reading the following guides making the part of ISO/IEC 25000 SQuaRE series [19]:

- ISO/IEC 25000—Guide to SQuaRE; provides the SQuaRE architecture model, terminology, documents overview, intended users, and associated parts of the series as well as reference models.

- ISO/IEC 25020—Measurement reference model and guide presents introductory explanation and a reference model that is common to quality measure elements, measures of internal software quality, external software quality, and quality in use.

Both TL9000 and ISO/IEC standards (9126 and 25000 series) offer the *process support* for identification, definition, measurement, and evaluation of software product quality. In the case of the TL9000 Quality Management System

Requirements Handbook, the support processes are located on the corporate level. In the case of ISO/IEC standards, the support is placed on the measurement process management level and is being offered through planning and management dedicated documents of ISO/IEC14598-2 and ISO/IEC 25001 [61].

The CQL model process does not need to be executed literally as presented, that is, starting from the discovery phase and ending with the operation and maintenance phase. It is the reader's decision at which point to enter and at which to exit the process, and thus which actions to undertake and execute and which to neglect. However, such a decision must take into consideration the following issues:

- When entering the process at a point different than the discovery phase, the user takes the risk of omitting (or neglecting) the operational quality requirements and quality in use requirements in software product quality definition. This may severely reduce the final quality of a software product.

- Entering the process at any point different than the discovery phase may reduce flexibility of iterations within the model.

REFERENCES

1. Pfleeger SL, Atlee JM. *Software Engineering: Theory and practice*, 4th ed. Upper Saddle River, N.J.: Prentice Hall, 2009.
2. ABET. www.abet.org.
3. IEEE Standard 610.12. *IEEE Standard Glossary of Software Engineering Terminology*. New York: IEEE Computer Society, 1990.
4. Suryn W. "Ingénierie de la qualité logicielle." École de Technologie Supérieure, Montréal, Canada. Available at http://www.etsmtl.ca/Programmes-Etudes/Cours-horaires/Cours-horaires-cycles-sup/Fiche-de-cours?Sigle=MGL842.
5. Bourque P, Dupuis R, Abran A, Moore JW, Tripp L, Wolff S. "Fundamental Principles of Software Engineering: A Journey." *Journal of Systems and Software* 2002; 62: 59–70.
6. Pressman RS. *Software Engineering: A Practitioner's Approach*, 7th ed. New York: McGraw Hill, 2010.
7. ISO/IEC 9126-1 Software Engineering – Product Quality – Part 1: Quality Model. Geneva, Switzerland: International Organization for Standardization, 2001.
8. IEEE Standard 1061–1998. *IEEE Standard for a Software Quality Metrics Methodology*. New York: IEEE Computer Society, 1998.
9. Georgiadou E. "GEQUAMO: A Generic, Multilayered, Customizable, Software Quality Model." *Software Quality Control* 2003; 11(4):313–323.
10. Siaka, KV, Georgiadou E. "PERFUMES: A Scent of Product Quality Characteristics." 13th International Software Quality Management Conference; March 21–23, 2005, Gloucestershire, Cheltenham, UK.
11. Kitchenham B, Pfleeger SL. "Software Quality: The Elusive Target." *IEEE Software* 1996; 13(1):12–21.
12. McCall JA, Richards PK, Walters GF. "Factors in Software Quality." Rome Air Development Center Reports NTIS AD/A-049 014, NTIS AD/A-049 015 and NTIS AD/A-049

016. Griffiths Air Force Base, New York: Rome Air Development Center Air Force Systems Command.

13. Boehm BW, Brown JR, Kaspar JR, Lipow ML, *MacCleod G. Characteristics of Software Quality*. New York: American Elsevier, 1978.

14. Boehm BW, Brown JR, Lipow ML. "Quantitative Evaluation of Software Quality." In *2nd International Conference on Software Engineering, San Francisco*. San Francisco: IEEE Computer Society Press, 1976.

15. Dromey RG. "A Model for Software Product Quality." *IEEE Transactions on Software Engineering* 1995; 21:146–162.

16. ISO 9126-2 Software Engineering – Product Quality – Part 2: External Metrics. Geneva, Switzerland: International Organization for Standardization, 2003.

17. ISO 9126-3 Software Engineering – Product Quality – Part 3: Internal Metrics. Geneva, Switzerland: International Organization for Standardization, 2003.

18. ISO 9126-4 Software Engineering – Product Quality – Part 4: Quality in Use Metrics. Geneva, Switzerland: International Organization for Standardization, 2004.

19. ISO/IEC 25000 System and Software Engineering – SQuaRE – Software Product Quality Requirements and Evaluation. Geneva, Switzerland: International Organization for Standardization, 2005–2013.

20. ISO/IEC 25010 Systems and Software Engineering – Systems and Software Quality Requirements and Evaluation (SQuaRE) – System and Software Quality Models. Geneva, Switzerland: International Organization for Standardization, 2011.

21. ISO/IEC 15939 Systems and Software Engineering – Measurement Process. Geneva, Switzerland: International Organization for Standardization, 2007.

22. ISO/IEC 25020 Systems and Software Engineering – Systems and Software Quality Requirements and Evaluation (SQuaRE) – Measurement Reference Model and Guide. Geneva, Switzerland: International Organization for Standardization, 2007.

23. ISO/IEC 25040 Systems and Software Engineering – Systems and Software Quality Requirements and Evaluation (SQuaRE) – Evaluation Process. Geneva, Switzerland: International Organization for Standardization, 2011.

24. ISO/IEC 14598-1 Information Technology – Software Product Evaluation – Part 1: General Overview. Geneva, Switzerland: International Organization for Standardization, 1999.

25. ISO 15288 Systems and Software Engineering – System Life Cycle Processes. Geneva, Switzerland: International Organization for Standardization, 2008.

26. ISO 25022 Systems and Software Engineering – Systems and Software Quality Requirements and Evaluation (SQuaRE) – Measurement of Quality in Use. Geneva, Switzerland: International Organization for Standardization; document in development.

27. ISO 25023 Systems and Software Engineering – Systems and Software Quality Requirements and Evaluation (SQuaRE) – Measurement of System and Software Product Quality. Geneva, Switzerland: International Organization for Standardization, document in development.

28. ISO/IEC 14598-3 Software Engineering – Product Evaluation – Part 3: Process for Developers. Geneva, Switzerland: International Organization for Standardization, 2000.

29. ISO/IEC 14598-4 Software Engineering – Product Evaluation – Part 4: Process for Acquirers. Geneva, Switzerland: International Organization for Standardization, 1999.

30. ISO/IEC 14598-5 Information Technology – Software Product Evaluation – Part 5: Process for Evaluators. Geneva, Switzerland: International Organization for Standardization, 1998.

31. ISO 25041 Systems and Software Engineering – Systems and Software Quality Requirements and Evaluation (SQuaRE) – Evaluation Guide for Developers, Acquirers and Independent Evaluators. Geneva, Switzerland: International Organization for Standardization, 2012.

32. ISO 14598-6 Software Engineering – Product Evaluation – Part 6: Documentation of Evaluation Modules. Geneva, Switzerland: International Organization for Standardization, 2001.

33. ISO 25042 Systems and Software Engineering – Systems and Software Quality Requirements and Evaluation (SQuaRE) – Evaluation Modules. Geneva, Switzerland: International Organization for Standardization, document in development.

34. Abran A, Moore JW, Bourque P, Dupuis R, editors. *Guide to the Software Engineering Body of Knowledge*, 2004. Los Alamitos: IEEE Computer Society, 2004.

35. Suryn W, Abran A. ISO/IEC SQuaRE. "The Second Generation of Standard for Quality of Software Products." 7th IASTED International Conference on Software Engineering and Applications, November 3–5, 2003. Marina del Rey, 2003.

36. Robertson S, Robertson J. *Mastering the Requirements Process*. Addison-Wesley, 1999.

37. *TL9000 Quality Management System Measurements Handbook, Release 3.0*. Plano: QuEST Forum, 2001.

38. ISO 25030 Systems and Software Engineering – Systems and Software Quality Requirements and Evaluation (SQuaRE) – Quality Requirements. Geneva, Switzerland: International Organization for Standardization, 2007.

39. Dai L, Cooper K. "Modeling and Analysis of Non-functional Requirements as Aspects in a UML Based Architecture Design." *6th International Conference on Software Engineering, Artificial Intelligence, Networking and Parallel/Distributed Computing and First ACIS International Workshop on Self-Assembling Wireless Networks, May 23–25, 2005*. Towson, WA: IEEE Computer Society. 2005, pp. 178–183.

40. Dai L, Cooper K. "Process Definition for the Formal Design Analysis Framework Creating an Aspect-Oriented Design Supporting Response Time Performance." Technical Report UTDCS-20-03. Department of Computer Science, University of Texas, Dallas, 2003.

41. Dai L, Cooper K. "Helping to Meet the Security Needs of Enterprises: Using FDAF to Build RBAC into Software Architectures." In *5th International Workshop on System/Software Architecture, June 27, 2006*, Las Vegas, pp. 790–796.

42. Cooper K, Dai L, Deng Y. "Performance Modeling and Analysis of Software Architectures: An Aspect-Oriented UML Based Approach." *Journal of Science of Computer Programming, System and Software Architectures* 2005; 57(1):89–108.

43. Herrman A, Paech B. "MOQARE: Misuse-Oriented Quality Requirements Engineering." *Requirements Engineering Journal* 2007; 13(1):73–86.

44. Herrmann A, Kerkow D, Doerr J. *Exploring the Characteristics of NFR Methods- A Dialogue about Two Approaches*. Berlin: Springer Verlag, 2007, pp. 320–334.

45. Kazman R, Klein M, Clements P. "ATAM: Method for Architecture Evaluation." Technical Report CMU/SEI-2000-TR-004. Software Engineering Institution, Carnegie Mellon University.

46. Dörr J, Kerkow D, Koenig T, Olsson T, Suzuki T. "Non-functional Requirements in Industry: Three Case Studies Adopting an Experience-based NFR Method." In *13th IEEE International Requirements Engineering Conference; August 29–September 2, 2005*, Paris, pp. 373–384.

47. Chung L, Nixon BA. "Dealing with Non-functional Requirements: Three Experimental Studies of a Process-Oriented Approach." In *17th International Conference on Software Engineering, April 24–28, 1995*. Seattle, WA: IEEE, 1995.

48. Chung L, Nixon BA, Yu E. "Using Quality Requirements to Systematically Develop Quality Software." 4th International Conference on Software Quality; October 3–5, 1994, McLean.

49. Djouab R, Suryn W. "SOQUAREM: Software Quality Requirements Engineering Method." 19th International Software Quality Management Conference, April 18–20, 2011. Loughborough University, UK, 2011.

50. Djouab R, Suryn W. "Applicability of SOQUAREM Method: An Illustrative Case Study." 19th International Software Quality Management Conference, April 18–20, 2011. Loughborough University, UK, 2011.

51. Business Rules Group 2007. "Business Motivation Model Version 1.3." Available at http://www.businessrulesgroup.org/actvbrg.shtml.

52. Côté MA, Suryn W, Martin R, Laporte CY. "Evolving a Corporate Software Quality Assessment Exercise: A Migration Path to ISO/IEC 9126." *Software Quality Professional* 2004; 6(3):4–17.

53. Dutil D, Suryn W, Rose J, Thimot B. "Software Quality Engineering in the New ISO Standard: ISO/IEC 24748 – Systems and Software Engineering – Guide for Life Cycle Management." In *Third C* Conference on Computer Science and Software Engineering, May 19–21, 2010.* Montreal: Concordia University, 2010.

54. ISO/IEC 24748-1 Systems and Software Engineering – Life Cycle Management – Part 1: Guide for Life Cycle Management. Geneva, Switzerland: International Organization for Standardization, 2010.

55. ISO/IEC 17799 Information Technology – Security Techniques – Code of Practice for Information Security Management. Geneva, Switzerland: International Organization for Standardization, 2005.

56. McCabe T, Butler CW. "Design complexity measurement and testing." *ACM* 1989; 32(12):1415–1425.

57. ISOIEC 12207 Systems and Software Engineering – Software Life Cycle Processes. Geneva, Switzerland: International Organization for Standardization, 2008.

58. *A Guide to Project Management Body of Knowledge*, 5th ed. Project Management Institute, 2012.

59. ISO/IEC 10006: Quality Management – Guidelines to Quality in Project Management. Geneva, Switzerland: International Organization for Standardization, 1997.

60. Barbacci M, Jeromy Carriere S, Peter Feiler PH, Kazman R, Klein MH, Lipson HF, Longstaff TA, Weinstock CB. "Steps in an Architecture Tradeoff Analysis Method: Quality Attribute Models and Analysis." Technical report May 1998. Pittsburgh: SEI. Report number CMU/SEI-97-TR-029. Available from Software Engineering Institute, Carnegie Mellon University, Pittsburgh, www.sei.cmu.edu.

61. ISO 25001 Systems and Software Engineering – Systems and Software Quality Requirements and Evaluation (SQuaRE) – Planning and Management. Geneva, Switzerland: International Organization for Standardization, 2007.

Chapter 3

System and Software Quality Engineering: Some Application Contexts

This chapter discusses software quality engineering in the application context of two categories of software systems: the information systems subcategory of information management, and embedded systems. Such a choice is based on their presence and/or the importance they bear in everyday social life. Information management systems, no matter their size and complexity, are present in almost every domain of social life. They can be found in libraries, hospitals, big international corporations, small enterprises, governments, or military institutions. Embedded systems are present in the life of almost every individual on the planet. They reside in wristwatches, microwave ovens, TVs, chip credit cards, cars, and planes, but also in missile guidance systems, nuclear reactor controllers, and nuclear missiles.

And a practical remark: even if the choice is limited to only two categories, the approach used in both cases is valid for any other category of software or system.

3.1 SOFTWARE QUALITY ENGINEERING IN THE INFORMATION MANAGEMENT SYSTEMS ENVIRONMENT

Information management systems are systems that help the users better exploit and understand the information remaining in their access. In this book, the word "access" is understood as *legal* access. As the concept, information management systems were first developed by IMB in 1968 and consisted of two layers, database system and transaction system (the interested reader can follow this story on the IBM Website). In fact, this basic structure still makes up the backbone of most contemporary information management systems. This type of system can perform multiple tasks such as document management, knowledge management, customer relationship

Software Quality Engineering: A Practitioner's Approach, First Edition. Witold Suryn.
© 2014 the Institute of Electrical and Electronics Engineers, Inc.
Published 2014 by John Wiley & Sons, Inc.

management, and enhanced collaboration throughout the organization. Usually these systems also provide some deep administration and integration capabilities, relevant search functionalities, as well as solid security features that protect the information they contain.

The information management systems represent what employees use to execute their daily tasks. Because of the amount of crucial business data they may contain, the *security* attribute seems very important. Businesses simply cannot allow these data to fall into the wrong hands. Further down that line, the data processed by these systems may vary from memos to employees to sensitive financial or production information, where, in the latter case, the *accuracy* is a feature that conditions the results of related operations. Finally, since not every employee is an IT-savvy user, it seems recommendable that these systems be user-friendly, which means *operable* and customizable.

Security, as defined in ISO 25010 [1], means the "degree to which a product or system protects information and data so that persons or other products or systems have the degree of data access appropriate to their types and levels of authorization." This quality characteristic has five subcharacteristics (the definitions come from ISO/IEC 25010):

- Confidentiality: degree to which a product or system ensures that data are accessible only to those authorized to have access
- Integrity: degree to which a system, product, or component prevents unauthorized access to, or modification of, computer programs or data
- Nonrepudiation: degree to which actions or events can be proven to have taken place, so that the events or actions cannot be repudiated later
- Accountability: degree to which the actions of an entity can be traced uniquely to the entity
- Authenticity: degree to which the identity of a subject or resource can be proved to be the one claimed.

What might happen if these quality attributes were not engineered into the system or software, or were not effective enough?

The absent *confidentiality* may lead to breaking the informational, social, and operational structure of an organization. Letting *anybody* access *anything* could disclose a company's confident data (including trade secrets), personal files of employees, plans, or strategies, causing a catastrophe that would paralyze the organization functioning for good and for a long time.

The *integrity*, as understood by ISO/IEC 25010, leads to connotations of industrial espionage and sabotage. In fact, missing *integrity* would allow someone properly prepared to access the organization's information management system's data and play with it according to his or her goals. The next day it might happen that the competition knows how to build the company's secret new product, but the company do not know how to do it, because all the plans and designs were deleted from their system. Actually, the latter is a bit overdramatized, for the companies that have important secrets keep them in several secured places.

Nonrepudiation and *accountability* refer to "I did not do it" types of situations. In information management it is important to know with a required level of certainty who sent the information and, if the consequences of this action are in any sense "special," to be able to trace it back (with a convincing proof) to the entity responsible for it and make him or her accountable. The value of these attributes is true both in internal and external exchange of information, but is this importance critical? The false information sent by a fake entity, if convincingly wrapped, may invoke harming actions, even chaos, but still it will not be similar to what may be created by missing confidentiality or integrity.

The *authenticity* of the data circulating in an organization's information management system is important principally from the decision making point of view. In simple terms, making decisions based on unverified information may, but does not have to, lead to incorrect decisions. Depending on the importance of these decisions the consequences may be marginal or catastrophic, as when stock exchange operations are based on rumors.

Accuracy, replaced in ISO/IEC 25010 by *functional correctness* (a subcharacteristic of the *functional suitability* characteristic of dynamic/external quality) is defined as the "degree to which a product or system provides the correct results with the needed degree of precision." Those readers who sometimes watch the news from the stock exchange have surely noticed that the exchange ratios between currencies sometimes go to the precision of one hundredth of a cent. The reason for such an exceptional precision is the quantity of money that flows through the stock exchange every day. If a transaction of $100 was supposed to be done with 0.01% (one hundredth of a cent) precision, but due to low accuracy attribute was performed with 1% (one cent) precision, the resulting sum instead of being $100 ± 1¢ would be $100 ± $1. Not a big tragedy on this level of sums, but for a transaction of $100 million, such an error might result in $1 million loss. So this explains the need for precision, but there is also "degree to which a product or system provides the correct results." The "degree" illustrates number of operations that were executed with poor precision against the total number of operations under test, so "the smaller, the better." If this degree exhibited by an information management system is close to zero, the system is considered of the appropriate *functional correctness*. The further it goes from zero value, the less this quality attribute is present in the system or software and, depending on the importance and type of its usage, the repercussion may vary from negligible to grave.

The *operability*, understood as the "degree to which a product or system has attributes that make it easy to operate and control" (ISO/IEC 25010), exhibits its importance especially on the level of employee adaptation to the system or software and, in consequence, on the resulting effectiveness of their work. Customizability makes a logical extension of operability, for which the two basic justifications could be:

- Organizations using information management systems are highly diversified, so their employee needs are not exactly the same and the system should allow not only for easy operation but for required adaptations as well

- In the era of globalization of businesses, the organizations tend to have offices in different regions of the planet, so both operability and customizability may play a key role in quick and effective setup of theses offices.

It should be understood that the aforementioned information management system quality attributes were chosen as commonly recognized for this category of IT systems, so the recommendations presented this chapter are naturally nonexhaustive. In real life cases these attributes could be analyzed as the first, but, for the sake of the final quality of the developed system or software, should rather not be the only ones taken into consideration.

3.2 SOFTWARE QUALITY ENGINEERING IN AN EMBEDDED SYSTEMS ENVIRONMENT

Embedded systems make quite often the invisible part of everyday life of most people around the globe. The majority of modern appliances contain a box where some smart microprocessor executes lines of code to control the required process. But also much less harmless or safe instruments contain embedded systems that control their behavior. And while some flaw in laundry washer software quality may create a red stain on your new shirt, a similar flaw in a missile-guiding system may cost human lives.

A common perception of an embedded system is a "closed system." Today it is and is not true at the same time. The system that contains an assembly code burnt into PROM definitely is not an open one and any active operation on it would require having it installed somewhere outside its natural environment. But if some change should be needed in software residing in a Java card (a microchip credit card with Java Virtual Machine and service applets) it can be done directly inside the chip through the appropriate application programming interface (API). The same can be said about cellular phones, so are they still embedded systems or just "very micro" but nonetheless open systems?

This question may be answered through the basic analysis of the features of the existing incarnations of embedded systems. A *closed embedded system* is characterized by:

- Development: outside the actual device
- Testing:
  - inside the device—"black box" only
  - if "white box" required—outside the device in emulated/simulated environment
- Maintenance: outside the actual device *only*.

So, naturally, an *open embedded system* would allow for:

- Development: *principally* outside the actual device
- Testing: "white box" and "black box" possible
- Maintenance: inside and outside the actual device.

Why is it so important to know how open a given embedded system is? Because:

- Evaluation of quality requires measurement
- Measurement requires an access to both the code and the behavior of the embedded system (also on the level of the available stimuli)
- Evaluation of quality invokes engineering decisions
- Engineering decisions for their realization often require physical manipulation of the embedded system
- Level of openness impacts the effectiveness of manipulations and, as such, the required quality engineering results.

This list may and should invoke a very important methodological question: if the fact of the system being *embedded* influences so severely the technical means of engineering the quality into it, are the available quality-related tools applied for nonembedded systems usable at all in the embedded systems case? Before this question is answered, the quality-related tools applied for nonembedded systems should be identified. The quality engineer's toolbox consists of at least four sets of instruments:

- quality model
- quality measures and related measurement methods and techniques
- evaluation methods and techniques
- engineering models, processes, and best practices.

Returning to the question "are the available quality-related tools applied for open systems usable at all in embedded systems case?" one might be tempted to answer "no," arguing that "an embedded system is too closed and machine-dependent to allow for elaborate manipulations required by quality engineering." A plausible answer, but not the only one possible. The second, equally plausible answer could be "perhaps," as ISO/IEC 9126 and ISO/IEC 25000 state in their text that "characteristics defined are applicable to every kind of software, including computer programs and data contained in firmware." Finally, there is also a firm "yes." In order to prove the practical value of this answer, the activities presented in Fig. 3.1 should be taken into consideration.

As the main real difference between embedded and nonembedded systems that matters is the level of their "closeness," the most important activity required in order to fully apply available quality engineering techniques is to "unclose" them (through the appropriate transformation environment [TE]). This "unclosure" will allow the internal/static quality engineering (the engineering on the level of developing the source code) to be executed. External/dynamic quality and quality in use are usually decided in the design phase and evaluated when the code is actually run, so there is no need for external or in use quality-dedicated TE. The eventual interventions that may result from this higher-level evaluation of quality will have to be engineered into the code, in which case the existing TE shall be applied. In conclusion, the available quality engineering tools and methods are generally applicable to most of

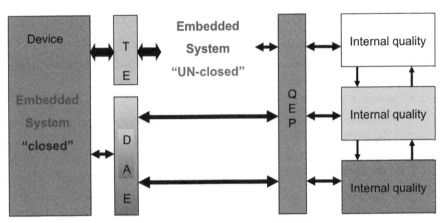

Figure 3.1   Adaptation of quality engineering processes to embedded systems.

known types of software, even if they may require some adjustments in the development environment, but none of these adjustments create obstacles justifying negligence in engineering quality into developed embedded software.

As in any type of software, the final result is perceived through the lenses of functionality and quality. There is no real user who would accept a software system, embedded or not, having a panoply of functionalities but missing the required quality (e.g., safety or reliability). On the other hand, it would probably still be possible to convince a user to accept a software product with limited set of functionalities but exhibiting excellent quality. In other words, quality is as important for embedded systems as it is for general purpose ones. Or is it more important?

Before answering this question, it may be profitable to first analyze the areas of application of embedded software or system. Some commonly recognized applicability contexts may be defined as follows [2, 3]:

- Mobile computing
- Multimedia
- Telecom
- Automotive
- Avionics
- Industrial control and sensors
- Consumer electronics and appliance
- Military
- Health
- Space technology.

A quick analysis will immediately reveal that some of these applications are potentially more harmful than the others (such as military or health), which in turn invokes the notion of *criticality*. The criticality of a system can be defined in the following way: "A critical system is integral to the proper running of an operation. If a critical application fails for any length of time the result may be catastrophic, including loss of life, serious injury, platform or mission failure, operational chaos or even bankruptcy."

Commonly recognized categories of embedded systems such as real-time interrupt-driven (RTID), mission-, or business-critical [2, 3] each have their sets of characteristics that position them on the scale of criticality, however, such a classification is not complete enough to cover the most important criticality areas. In fact, a vaster categorization would be required to identify those that are most prone to missing quality. Such a categorization would consist of:

- Real-time interrupt-driven (RTID)
- Mission-critical
- Business-critical
- Safety-critical
- Security-critical.

When matching the aforementioned categories against the applicability fields of embedded systems a categorization matrix can be created (Table 3.1).

How exactly can one identify the impact of missing quality on the criticality of a given embedded system? Can it be predicted, measured, foreseen? If so, are the software engineers able to control and manipulate it?

The first thing that comes to mind when analyzing the impact of quality on the criticality of the embedded system is the analogy to the risk impact, understood in its classic definition. In simple terms, less quality means more risk, which, if applied to the criticality of an embedded system, translates into making its user more vulnerable than he or she would be if quality was there or, in an extreme case, pushing the embedded system to an "explosion area" (Fig. 3.2). To help us better understand this analogy, three fictive examples are discussed in the following:

- Very high criticality: an on-board control system of a missile
- High criticality: automotive—an on-board control system a vehicle
- Low criticality: appliance—an on-board control system of a washing machine.

Table 3.1 Embedded Systems Categorization Matrix

Application Category	Mobile Comp.	Multi media	Tele com	Auto motive	Avio nics	Health	Industrial Control	Consumer Appliances	Space	Military
RTID							X	X		
Business	X	X	X	X	X	X			X	
Mission	X		X		X	X			X	X
Safety				X	X	X	X	X	X	X
Security						X			X	X

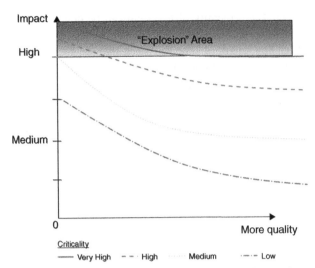

Figure 3.2   Illustration of the impact of quality on criticality of an embedded system.

In all three cases, the quality attribute of *restorability* (the subcharacteristic of recoverability, the characteristic of reliability) has been measured. In ISO/IEC 9126-2 the attribute of *restorability* is defined as the "ability of the system to restore itself properly after an abnormal event." When analyzing theoretically the impact of low restorability in each of the three examples, one will inevitably come to the following simple conclusions:

- The missile case: if restorability is low, then the probability of an uncontrolled explosion becomes high
- The vehicle case: if restorability is low, the driver may have an accident
- The washing machine case: if restorability is low, then the probability of having dirty laundry becomes high.

In order to further analyze the most interesting example of the three, the missile, the "obtained" (measured) attribute of restorability has had the value set up at 0.5, which means that the embedded control system was able to "intelligently reboot" and restore itself in half of all observed cases. In other words, the probability of the manifestation (PM) of a wrong restore operation of the missile control system is 50%. For a missile, it looks really bad; however, there is a second condition that may moderate the severity of the situation: the occurrence of the stimulus (disturbance) that would make the control system restore (probability of disturbance, PD). In verbal form, the prediction of the impact of the restorability 0.5 could sound as follows: half of missiles having this embedded system on board will end up badly *if unexpected disturbance* requiring a restore operation *occurs*.

This expression can be translated into a classic, risk evaluation-based notation:

(1) IP $=$ PM $\times$ PD

(2) Risk Exposure $=$ IP $\times$ Consequences (like cost or loss of human life)

Where IP: Impact Prediction; PM: Probability of Manifestation; PD: Probability of Disturbance.

To finally build the link between quality and its impact on criticality of an embedded system, the following facts must be taken into consideration:

- Impact on criticality $\approx$ Risk Impact (classical definition)
- Quality is measurable (quantitative), as there exist:
  ○ applicable quality models (McCall, Boehm, ISO/IEC 9126, ISO 25010)
  ○ associated quality measures (ISO/IEC 9126, ISO/IEC 25022, ISO/IEC 25023, when published)
  ○ evaluation methods and techniques (ISO/IEC 14598, ISO/IEC 25040, ISO/IEC 25041, ISO/IEC 2504, when published)
- Quality is definable (qualitative)
- Applying quality engineering methods allows for identifying (critical and noncritical) technical elements of real quality of given software
- Level of quality and known technical data should allow for measuring the impact (the available technical data shall be representative to the case).

The resulting impact prediction process that encapsulates both quality evaluation and the probability of the occurrence of the source event (the "unexpected disturbance") is shown in Fig. 3.3.

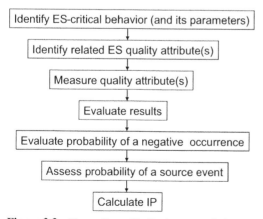

Figure 3.3   The quality–criticality impact prediction process.

Using the aforementioned approach in the process of choosing quality attributes relevant to a given embedded system or software could help identify the ones that are critical to the context in which the system is being used, and by doing so, through the proper engineering activities limit the probability and potential effects of its harmful behavior.

From a practical perspective, the choice of real instruments from quality engineer's toolbox mentioned earlier in this chapter is rather limited. Among all known quality models, at the moment of writing this book, only ISO/IEC 9126 comes with associated measures and recommendations for measurement techniques (its modernized replacement ISO/IEC 25000 SQuaRE series is still not completed).

This model and its measures are accompanied by the complementary set of standards, the "sister" standard ISO/IEC 14598 (or, in case of ISO/IEC 2502x, the standards from ISO/IEC 2504x division), which offer support for quality management and evaluation, which altogether makes the only widely known complete toolset for quality evaluation.

As for quality engineering models, processes, and practices, the choice of tools is also limited, with one of them being publicly available as the SQIM model discussed in details in Section 2.3.1.

The criticality analysis presented earlier, as well as the commonly recognized applicability contexts discussed in this chapter, help identify and choose the quality characteristics (attributes) that would most frequently be recognized as "important" for embedded software or systems. They were identified as: *fault tolerance, recoverability, reliability, accuracy,* and *security.*

Fault tolerance is defined in ISO/IEC 25010 as the "degree to which a system, product or component operates as intended despite the presence of hardware or software faults." Its importance may be neglected in case of a washing machine, but for a missile guidance system this quality attribute is critical.

Recoverability is defined in ISO/IEC 25010 as the "degree to which, in the event of an interruption or a failure, a product or system can recover the data directly affected and re-establish the desired state of the system." The importance of this quality attribute was proven earlier in this chapter, when the example of embedded systems in a missile, a car, and a washing machine were discussed.

Reliability is defined in ISO/IEC 25010 as the "degree to which a system, product or component performs specified functions under specified conditions for a specified period of time." This quality attribute is particularly important for embedded software that either interacts directly with living beings (e.g., medical life support equipment) or its failure has a direct and immediate impact on them (avionic, automotive, military). *Accuracy* and *security* were discussed in detail in Section 3.1.

Similarly to what was remarked in Section 3.2, it should be understood that the embedded system quality attributes discussed earlier were chosen as the most commonly recognized for this category of IT systems, so the recommendations presented this chapter are naturally nonexhaustive. In real-life cases, these attributes could be analyzed as the first, but for the sake of the final quality of the developed system or software, should not be the only ones taken into consideration.

REFERENCES

1. ISO/IEC 25010 Systems and Software Engineering—Systems and Software Quality Requirements and Evaluation (SQuaRE)—System and Software Quality Models. Geneva, Switzerland: International Organization for Standardization, 2011
2. Noergaard T. *Embedded Systems Architecture*. Amsterdam: Newnes, 2005.
3. Heath S. *Embedded Systems Design*. Oxford: Newnes, 2003.

Chapter 4

Trustworthiness of IT Systems and Services

4.1 WHAT IS TRUSTWORTHINESS IN THE IT DOMAIN?

The evolution of information technology and its products is one of the most rapid evolutions in the history of humanity. There are signals, from an IT evolution point of view, that we are fast approaching a trustworthiness critical entry point. Some indicators supporting this hypothesis are the IT market size and recent estimations on data quantities being processed globally. As can easily be found if one surfs patiently over the Internet, different sources give rather similar information:

- In 2006, the amount of digital information created, captured, and replicated was $1,288 \times 1,018$ bits. In computer parlance, that is 161 exabytes or 161 billion gigabytes. This is about 3 million times the information in all the books ever written.

- Between 2006 and 2010, the information added annually to the digital universe increased more than six-fold, from 161 exabytes to 988 exabytes.

All these enormous numbers make necessary two simple questions to be asked:

- What happens if only 0.001% of important information becomes untrustworthy?

- What happens if some of the systems involved in processing these data go "untrustworthy"?

The answer to these questions makes the most real raison d'être for intensified IT trustworthiness development efforts.

What *trustworthiness* means in the IT domain is the result of many decades of evolution of different, not always closely related sciences such as psychology, sociology, engineering, and even history. The widely known definition of trustworthiness applied in software engineering domain has been proposed and published in

Software Quality Engineering: A Practitioner's Approach, First Edition. Witold Suryn.
© 2014 the Institute of Electrical and Electronics Engineers, Inc.
Published 2014 by John Wiley & Sons, Inc.

Reference 1 and is related to conformance to requirements: "An entity is trustworthy if there is sufficient credible evidence leading one to believe that the system will meet a set of given requirements. Trust is a measure of trustworthiness, relying on the evidence provided."

The notion of trustworthiness applied in human relationships is being continuously discussed on different open fora, with one of the most interesting perspectives published on Wikipedia [2]: "Trustworthiness is a moral value considered to be a virtue. A trustworthy person is someone in whom we can place our trust and rest assured that the trust will not be betrayed."

The records of the Minnesota State Archives [3] give a very succinct yet precise illustration of what trustworthiness may mean for the history: "[Trustworthiness] refers to the reliability and authenticity of records."

Finally, the linguistic definition related to *engineering* that can be found in most online and printed dictionaries is: "Trustworthiness is an attribute of an entity deserving of trust or confidence, being dependable and reliable."

The key notions that can be withdrawn as a common denominator from all the above definitions are: reliability, credibility, and dependability. And, in the essence, they represent the lion's share of what a contemporary IT user (consumer) would expect from software or system that processes his or her *sensitive* information. However, to be true to the reality, to present a twenty-first century user's perception of trustworthiness, a larger list of attributes must be drawn:

- Quality
- Reliability
- Credibility
- Dependability
- Completeness of required functions
- Proper quality–cost ratio (so the software was not overpaid)
- Post-sale maintenance and service
- Pre- and post-sale training
- Documentation
- Responsibility for the product.

Some of these elements may seem secondary in comparison with, for example, quality or dependability, but the real market shows cases where suppliers have lost the trust of their customers after offering "lousy" post-sale support.

The introduction of the Internet and wireless broadband networks together with service-oriented architectures has facilitated the composition of interactive services using web technologies and web communities.

The interrelationships and interdependencies between formerly stand-alone systems and networks are leading to complexities in the infrastructures of our society that have never been seen before. These complex systems and networks have access to massive amounts of personal and business data, information, and content in ways that are difficult for users to understand and control. In recent years we have witnessed a growing series of accidents and attacks on the Internet and on applications and databases. Through service attacks, viruses, phishing, spyware, and other malware, criminals disrupt service provisioning and steal personal or confidential business data for financial gain or other purposes. These disruptive attacks impact the e-market on an international scale.

Apart from external attacks, there are also development-related causes for software to fail. Some of these are:

- Change of the program source code
- Modification of its context by updating libraries or changing its configuration
- Modification of its test suite.

Any of these changes can cause differences in program behavior and, as a result, influence the user's level of trust associated with it. A popular belief here is that the remedy for losing the user's trust is *tests*.

Software testing is a way to find faults in software. It is a process of supplying a system under test with some values and making conclusions on the basis of its behavior. The most significant weakness of testing is that the functioning of the tested system can, in principle, only be verified for those input situations that were selected as test data. According to Dijkstra [4], testing can only show the existence but not the nonexistence of errors. Proof of correctness can only be produced by a complete test, that is, a test with all possible input values, input value sequences, and input value combinations under all practically possible constraints, which is theoretically possible but unfeasible in practice. In conclusion, tests are one of crucial components in building software or system trustworthiness, but alone are not enough.

The literature related to trust and software trustworthiness attributes and factors mentions several different approaches, with few of them presented briefly in the following. The National Science and Technology Council (NSTC) in the United States concentrates on high confidence systems and cyber-physical systems that are categorized into physical, biological, and engineered systems whose operations are integrated, monitored, and/or controlled by a computational core. Components are networked at every scale. Computing is "deeply embedded" into every physical component, possibly even into materials. The computational core is an embedded system, usually demanding real-time response, and is most often distributed. The behavior of a cyber-physical system is a fully integrated hybridization of computational (logical) and physical action [5]. In this category, the emphasis is on safety, stability, and performance attributes.

Avizienis et al. have defined dependability as the reliance that can justifiably be placed on the service that the system delivers [6]. Dependability has become an important aspect of computer systems since everyday life increasingly depends on software. Although there is a large body of research in dependability, architectural level reasoning about dependability is only just emerging as an important theme in software engineering. This is due to the fact that dependability concerns are usually left until too late in the process of development. Additionally, the complexity of emerging applications and the trend of building trustworthy systems from existing untrustworthy components are urging dependability concerns to be considered at the architectural level. Lemos et al. have recognized fault prevention, fault removal, fault tolerance, and fault forecasting as important quality attributes for dependable systems [7].

A group of multinational technology and consulting firms such as HP, IBM, Intel, and Microsoft have formed the Trusted Computing Platform Alliance (TCPA) [8]. Their belief is that the totality (hardware, firmware, software) of the components is responsible for enforcing a security policy so that the system operates as expected. The group eventually grew to over 190 members and focused on "improving trust and security on computing platforms." Later, TCPA was replaced by the Trusted Computing Group (TCG) that concentrates on hardware and software security and use of cryptography in maintaining security.

Microsoft has developed an integrated process called trustworthy computing for improving the security of commercial software as it is being developed. Microsoft believes that there are three facets for building more secure software: repeatable process, engineer education, and metrics and accountability [9]. In Microsoft's experience, the benefits of providing more secure software (e.g., fewer patches, more satisfied customers) outweigh the costs.

The Trusted Computer National Evaluation Criteria (TCNEC) restricted trustworthiness based on security as the only attribute to consider [10]. Parnas et al. define software trustworthiness as level of appropriateness of using software engineering techniques to reduce failure rates, including techniques to enhance testing, reviews, and inspections [11]. In the study of Trustworthy Software Methodology (TSM) originally performed by the US National Security Agency, software trustworthiness was defined as "the degree of confidence that exists to meet a set of requirements."

The Data and Analysis Center for Software (DACS) has produced two reports, Software Assurance for Project Management [12] and Software Security Assurance [13]. In the former, the researchers emphasized that software trustworthiness factors and metrics are only restricted to the project management-related factors and metrics, while in the latter the focus is on security assurance for measuring software trustworthiness and they used a number of security-enhanced software methodologies such as Microsoft's Trustworthy Computing SDL.

There are also works discussed in the next sections that develop trustworthiness structures based entirely on the notions of quality and applying as its framework the ISO/IEC 9126 set of standards. As can be seen, the perception of trustworthiness and related concepts vary from one organization or researcher to another and all of them are in some sense partial.

Before going further into the details of the contemporary positioning of trustworthiness, it may be profitable to shortly repaint the actual IT market diversity. *OTS (off-the-shelf)* applications enjoy the biggest population of users. In this category we find, among others, software that supports individual tasks or set of tasks such as text editing, media processing and playing, individual accountancy or finance, some data processing, and simple database applications. Using such software usually does not require specific IT knowledge but rather some self-learning about how to use it and eventually adapt it to our needs.

Commercial Modular Systems (CMS) are built from predeveloped modules or subsystems for a known user, having large, configurable, yet finished set of functionalities. In most cases, functionalities are linked together into "services." The user population is mostly corporate and as such requires intensive training before becoming fully operational and productive. The training may be divided into end-user type, which is service-oriented, and technical user training, which goes into the category of operation and maintenance. In both cases, the training is done by the supplier or his or her delegated representatives (certified companies). One of the best-known examples would be the ERP type of IT systems.

Individual On-Demand Systems (IOS) are developed to meet individual and unique requirements of the known user. The system may offer functionalities, services, or both. As in case of a CMS, the user population is mostly corporate and in consequence also requires intensive training. The training types are similar too, that is, they may be divided into end-user and technical-user training, but are done by the supplier only, as the supplier is usually is the only source of knowledge available to the user.

What do all these applications/systems have in common?

- The user owns them (or at least the license to use them)
- The user knows how build them
- The user knows whom to pursue (or sue) if something goes wrong
- The trustworthiness in this context is manageable, as the responsibility can be pinpointed to a known entity.

The last statement is a bit of wishful thinking, for actual legal and market ramifications make the fight of an individual consumer against an IT giant very difficult at best. However, the framework is there, which means that there is a known entity (a supplier) that can be reached and made accountable for its actions. Except we are not there yet. This aspect becomes even more disputable if the recent developments in IT domain are taken into consideration. For some years now there are two buzzwords that excite both suppliers and IT consumers, not necessarily for the same reasons: service-oriented architecture and cloud computing.

Service-Oriented Architecture (SOA) is essentially a collection of services. These services communicate with each other in order to establish the cooperation that can involve two or more services coordinating some activity in order to "do a job." The technology of Web services is the most likely connection technology of service-oriented architecture. The idea by itself is not necessarily very new, as its younger, less "fancy" predecessors such as DCOM or CORBA have been well known for a few decades now. The user's position in regard of trustworthiness is in such a case "undefined" at best, as there is no "named entity" that could eventually be linked to the service as a whole. In other words, there is no one to blame within a given SOA structure for eventual losses that the consumer has suffered.

Cloud computing is a general term for anything that involves delivering hosted services over the Internet. These services are broadly divided into three categories: Infrastructure as a Service (IaaS), Platform as a Service (PaaS), and Software as a Service (SaaS). *IaaS* is simply a virtual server instance with a unique IP address and blocks of storage on demand that can be used by the customer as it suits him or her. *PaaS* represents a set of software and product development tools hosted on the provider's infrastructure that allow the customer create his or her own application or even system. *SaaS* is a vendor-supplied hardware and software product infrastructure that interacts with the user through a front-end portal. The user's position in regard to trustworthiness in these three categories of services seems to be a bit more controllable, as there is a "vendor" or "supplier" who can theoretically be linked to the given service, but in fact the user may easily fall into a modern version of a classic "dot com" pattern. All these "vendors" and "suppliers" are no more than virtual entities, hidden somewhere in the "cloud" of the Internet, never seen, never talked to, practically out of any direct control.

So what could or would be a twenty-first century IT user's perception of trustworthiness in an era of *cloud computing* or *SOA*? It can be analyzed in a rather speculative way from the perspective of trustworthiness attributes discussed earlier, although the obtained results most probably would be too general for a particular IT consumer. Instead, it would be recommended that the user, before deciding whether a given application/service/system potentially exhibits required trustworthiness, analyze as precisely as possible the known trustworthiness attributes by answering the few related questions listed in the following:

- Quality. Of what? Service, system, SOA sub-services, PaaS?
- Reliability. (Same as the above.)
- Credibility. Whose credibility? Supplier's, vendor's, system's?
- Dependability. (Same as the above.)
- Completeness of required functions. In an era of SOA and cloud computing, are we still talking about "functionalities"?
- Proper quality–cost ratio (so the software was nor overpaid). "How easy will it be to be verified in my particular case?"
- Post-sale maintenance and service. "What and how should and can be done in my particular case?"
- Pre- and post-sale training. (Same as the above.)
- Documentation. Who, what, and how should deliver?
- Responsibility for the product. Who represents the "product"?

4.2   ROLE OF IT TRUSTWORTHINESS IN CONTEMPORARY SOCIETY

Contemporary society has gradually become profoundly dependent on information technology. We are so used to its presence that it has become almost transparent, invisible, until something bad happens. Once it happens and once it is bad, the trust in our technological "servant" immediately diminishes. The existence of this lack of trust in information technology is known in the industry or we would not have backups, RAID solutions (redundant array of independent disks), redundant systems, and so on, however, the social objective of verifying the level of system or service trustworthiness goes far beyond mere technology. This objective is to assure a user in a proof-based way that he or she can trust the service (product, software) he or she wants or has to use. Obviously, if the developer puts a "you can trust it" stamp on his or her products no one will take it seriously, at least no one who lost data or hours of work trusting the "professionalism" of previously used software. Attribution of such a stamp should come from an independent, trusted, and professional entity having a good history of correct evaluations and should be a normal market practice.

The user could then, before buying a software product or service, verify the credibility of the supplier/producer, the quality of his or her services (meant here as, e.g., post-sale or customer support services) and seeing on the product a "you can trust it" stamp from the certification agency be relatively well assured that the risks of using it are reduced to an acceptable minimum.

This idea can be more precisely expressed through three practical domains of activities of a trustworthiness certification entity:

- Validation of IT solutions. This activity falls into the category "process for the evaluator" discussed in Section 4.3.2.2, and has as an objective to validate an IT solution on behalf of the future user. The "you can trust it" stamp, together with the exhaustive trustworthiness evaluation report, could serve, among others, as the crucial attachment to the main contract.
- Verification of IT suppliers. In this case, the certification could be applied to the supplier rather than to the product. In fact, not every "product" has to be software-based even if it exists in IT domain. The whole market of IT consultancy is based on services as products and the certified service supplier would be probably more sought after than an uncertified one.
- Certification of IT products and services. The whole market of OTS products and Internet-based (SOA, cloud computing) services would be the addressee of this part of a trustworthiness evaluation effort. The user then could choose between a box with a stamp that says "Trustworthiness Level y/10. Certified by National Trustworthiness Certification Agency. Valid until 20xx" and a box with no such stamp. The same could be applied to services, so the user would not be afraid that his or her sensitive data will begin its own quest in the labyrinth of the World Wide Web.

4.3 MONITORING, MEASUREMENT, AND CERTIFICATION OF IT TRUSTWORTHINESS

If the role of trustworthiness is to be effectively realized, at the base of this process there has to be an intellectually defendable and practically applicable understanding of what exactly constitutes trustworthiness in contemporary IT domain. Being a rather new technological concept, trustworthiness is under scientific scrutiny in several different ways, beginning with a quality-only static approach, through semi-dynamic, architecture-based solutions to dynamic, behavior-based measurement and evaluation process. These different perspectives are discussed further in the following sections.

4.3.1   Classic Approaches

The numbers quoted in previous section are widely known and acknowledged within the IT community. Several scientific efforts and research projects have been undertaken to tackle the problem of building the proper mechanisms (models, theories, methodologies) to allow for efficient estimation of trustworthiness of, generally speaking, information technology products. Same of them, such as the method proposed in Reference 14 (Fig. 4.1), the solution developed in Beijing University project "TRUSTIE" (Fig. 4.2) [15] or the methodology HATS (Highly Adaptable and Trustworthy Software Using Formal Models) [16] developed by Swedish Chalmers University of Technology (Fig. 4.3), have taken as their basis software quality measurement and evaluation approach represented in ISO/IEC 9126. As can be noticed, both models are parametrical, attribute-oriented, and heavily based on the ISO/IEC 9126 quality model.

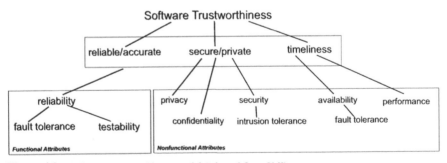

Figure 4.1   Software trustworthiness model (adapted from [14]).

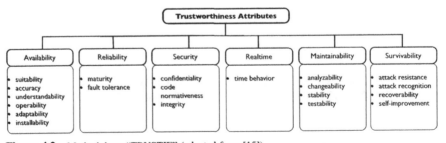

Figure 4.2   Methodology "TRUSTIE" (adapted from [15]).

Technological and Industrial Context of HATS

Software Dynamics: Adaptability
- Large software systems are extremely long-lived
- Variability: software must work in plethora of deployment scenarios
- Evolvability: frequent and unanticipated changes of requirements

Software Quality: Trustworthiness
- Nonfunctional aspects (security, resources) ever more important
- Challenges: product complexity, composability, concurrency
- Ensure and maintain intended behavior

Figure 4.3   HATS (adapted from [16]).

A relatively recent and rather innovative development is the dynamic, architecture-based solution, having two cooperating "engines": the trust engine and the auction engine [17]. The trust engine is "responsible for trust negotiation among services in order to establish the services that will be exchanged between the participating modules and set up a negotiated trust level for service access." The second "engine," the auction engine, is responsible for a computing trust level that the service provider has to prove. Once the trust level is bilaterally established and agreed upon, the whole service architecture may begin the realization of required tasks.

4.3.2 Dynamic Approaches: Behavioristic Method of Software, System, and Service Trustworthiness Certification

The notion of software trustworthiness evaluation in the literature is inherently subjective. It depends on how the software is used and in what context it is used. Moreover, different users evaluate a software system according to different criteria, point of view, and background. Therefore, when assessing software trustworthiness, it may be counterproductive to look for a general set of characteristics and parameters; instead, there is need to define a model that is tailored to the functional and quality requirements that the software has to fulfill. Such an approach is introduced in a behavioristic model for verifying software trustworthiness (BeMSET) based on scenarios of interactions between the software and its users and environment. These interactions consist of simple scenarios of examples or counterexamples of desired behavior. The approach supports incremental changes in requirements/scenarios.

4.3.2.1 General Concepts of the Method
The general concept behind the behavioristic approach to IT system or service trustworthiness is constructed on four basic points [18]:

- The final user does not want or have to be IT literate. He or she simply wants to be a *user.*

- The trust for a system or service does not have to be total. It is enough if it is *contextual*, that is, within the space of user's interests or needs.
- The behavior of a service/system in the given usage context can be represented in a formal way, applying one of the existing formal notation methods. In case of BeMSET, this notation is a combination of unified modeling language (UML) scenarios and finite state machine (FSM) computation model.
- The observed trends in information technology indicate that the distance between a consumer (user) of IT services and executive mechanisms necessary for these services grows.

The behavioral trustworthiness in order to fulfill its objectives as stated in Section 4.2 has to be supported by a process allowing for a transition from technical or descriptive expression of evaluation requirements (depending on the type and IT proficiency of the requester) to the documented results of evaluation and eventual issuance of a certificate.

Figure 4.4 presents such a framework process, a general model of BeMSET where the whole procedure is divided into six consecutive steps:

- *Identification of required scenarios/objects.* In this step the trustworthiness context and related usage scenarios are identified (example: context: online banking; scenario: transfer of funds from account A to account B).
- *Transformation of scenarios to their FSM representations.* In this step, the scenarios from Step 1 are transformed into FSM table(s) of states, transitions, and stimuli. This formal form of the service under evaluation is stored in a database for further processing and as part of the knowledge base for a given category of services.
- *Execution of scenarios by a real service or system.* In this step the scenarios from Step 1 are executed by a real system or service under evaluation. The states and transitions exhibited by it are recorded in FSM table(s) and stored in the database.
- *Comparison of transformed and recorded FSM tables.* This step applies mathematical methods of comparison of the two obtained FSM representations of the service or system under evaluation. As the result, the differences (deltas) in paths, states, and transitions between the real and required behavior of a system or service are found and documented.
- *Results evaluation.* This step has as an objective to qualitatively and quantitatively analyze the comparison results from the previous step. The applied analysis method (of the choice of the evaluator) should allow for classifying the discrepancies into at least three basic categories: fail, conditional pass, pass.
- *Issuance of the certificate.* The certificate must be based on a sound evaluation from the previous step and can be full, conditional, refused, one-time, renewable, periodic, or with no time limit. In case of a failed reevaluation,

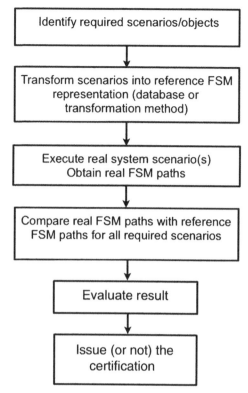

Figure 4.4   General model of BeMSET.

the certificate may also be revoked. All these cases should follow the rules established in and for a given certification authority.

In reality the BeMSET process is considerably more complex. In its form proposed in Reference 19, the process is built in three phases, each having several stages or steps (Fig. 4.5).

Phase 1: Identifying attributes of software or service trustworthiness. This phase is dedicated to identifying and characterizing the attributes and factors from user scenarios and/or UML scenarios. It is important to note that not only are the quality attributes that are important for the overall trustworthiness taken into account, but also the domain of software systems or services as well (see Section 1.2.3). The context of use is taken into consideration as the third perspective. It can be found out by answering the following questions:

- Who will use the software (users and roles)?
- What will be done with the software (functional requirements)?
- Where the software will be used (environment)?
- How will the software be used (quality requirements)?

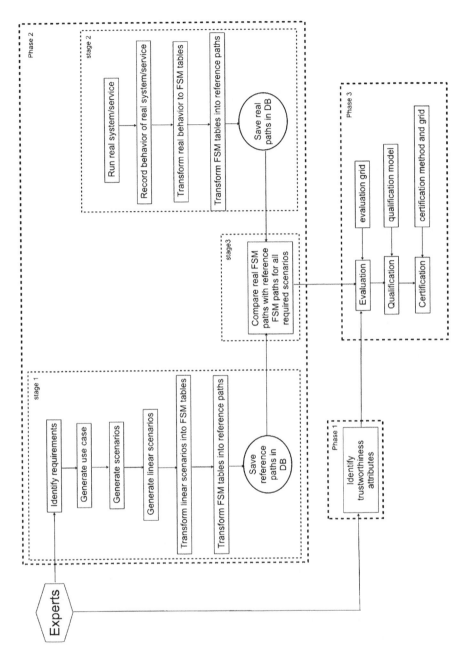

Figure 4.5 BeMSET trustworthiness evaluation process.

As the result, a generic list of all possible factors and attributes will be created and presented to the user. Then the user will choose those attributes and factors that relate and matter to the software system or service under investigation and will identify and define the properties of his or her interest. Therefore, the result of this phase is the definition of a generic model for factors and attributes of functional and/or quality requirements of a software system or services.

Phase 2: Developing a formal behavioristic model. In this phase, the selection (or development, if need be) of a formal specification language and the choice of a suitable formal notation (in case of BeMSET, FSM) for developing a formal behavioristic model are made. There are three stages and each stage has its own steps, as follows:

- Stage 1: Transforming reference requirements to FSM representation
  ○ identification of reference requirements
  ○ extraction of reference functionalities and quality attributes
  ○ generation of reference use cases
  ○ extraction of reference scenarios
  ○ transformation of any hierarchical (tree format) scenarios to nonhierarchical (linear format) scenarios
  ○ generation of reference FSM tables from each nonhierarchical (linear format) scenario
  ○ execution of reference FSM tables to obtain the reference path representation
  ○ saving reference path representation into reference database.

- Stage 2: Recording real software system or service behavior
  ○ execution of real software system or services
  ○ recording of the real behavior into real FSM tables
  ○ execution of real FSM tables and development of the real path representation
  ○ saving real path representation into the recording database.

- Stage 3: Comparing real behavior with reference behavior
  ○ reading real path representation from the recording database
  ○ reading reference path representation from the reference database
  ○ comparing reference path representation with real path representation
  ○ analyzing and interpreting the observed behavior and its discrepancy from reference behavior for the software system or services under investigation.

This mechanism of the model enables recording of paths of all the states, transitions, events, and actions in the sequence in which they are performed (real) or should have been performed (reference). These paths are saved in a database for future reference for both real and expected (reference) behavior of software system and services.

Phase 3: Evaluation method. In this phase, the analysis of the results of comparison between real FSM paths and reference FSM paths for all requested scenario(s) is executed. The evaluation of the results (whether the software system or services passed or not) is used as the basis for awarding (or not) the certification. The development or choice of the appropriate evaluation method of trustworthiness for software system or service under investigation is the most important part of this phase. For evaluation, all the information and results from Phase 1 and Phase 2 are taken into account. Also, the evaluation grid and qualification model are used to evaluate the behavior of software system or services. One other dimension of this phase is related to the interpretation of discrepancies between real behavior and reference behavior of software systems or services under investigation. The specific grids relate, among the others, to the category of the system or service under evaluation that should be used in certification process.

An additional remark about this process: let's keep in mind that the attributes and factors for trustworthiness of a system or software should be identified from user scenarios and/or UML scenarios. These attributes and factors contribute to analyzing and evaluating trustworthiness of the software system or service under investigation in a way shown in Fig. 4.6.

A scenario can be represented as a path consisting of state nodes and transition edges through the statechart diagram. Statechart diagrams have different types of actions that are performed within the state, such as [20]:

- Entry actions
- Input actions triggered by input conditions that do not cause state changes
- Exit actions

or cause state transitions, such as:

- Transition actions, which are a type of input action but are bound to a transition.

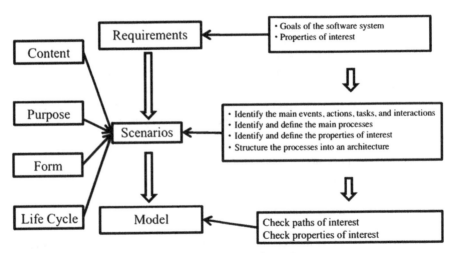

Figure 4.6 Views required to capture relevant aspects of scenarios.

A new scenario is written by adding states and state transitions to the state machine incrementally, in such a way that the requested scenario becomes executable as a path through the same statechart diagram. It should be noted that all those states and state transitions belong to the same use case. The following additional information is needed to generate a scenario and a statechart [21]:

- Any actions or events causing a trigger or state transitions such as clock events, pressing a button, or selecting a menu item
- Any action or events related to entering or choosing a data input or a change to data, such as completing a form or selecting a data item from a dropdown menu or trigger of timer or guard condition
- The object status of the system at the beginning state of scenario execution.

4.3.2.2   Service Trustworthiness Analysis and Certification

Let's recall that a basic definition of the adjective "trustworthy" uses the notion of "worthy of confidence" and "dependable" [22]. The term "trustworthiness" in the context of IT comes as the extrapolation of this definition and can be explained as "the assurance that a system deserves to be trusted, that it will perform as expected despite environmental disruptions, human and operator error, hostile attacks, and design and implementation errors" [23]. In real life, such an assurance is most often partial (or contextual) and needs to be evaluated using a stable and correct process and tangible data. The series of standards ISO 14598 provide the guidance and requirements for the evaluation process of software product quality from three different perspectives: development, acquisition, and an independent evaluation. It is also broadly known that quality makes an inherent component of trust, but equating it alone to trustworthiness would be considered a risky limitation of a trustworthiness concept. However, a practical question would be: Could the ISO/IEC 14598 evaluation processes be applied to evaluate trustworthiness, or it is necessary to develop something new? In light of the development of the ISO/IEC 25040, ISO/IEC 25041, and ISO/IEC 25042 standards dedicated to quality evaluation, the same question would apply to them. This possibility was analyzed using an example where an IT system was represented applying the behavioristic model of trustworthiness, BeMSET.

4.3.2.2.1   IT System Example

The IT system used in the analysis is a system for remote monitoring of diabetic patients in serious condition. In simple terms, a diabetic patient must connect each day before 10 a.m. to the system via its web portal, enter his or her blood sugar level, blood pressure, and weight, and submit these data for evaluation by the system. The basic functional requirements are then:

- The system shall collect patient's submitted data via its portal
- The system shall save the data in the medical history of the patient
- The system shall validate the collected data

- If the data represent a normal situation, the system shall wait for the next scheduled submission
- Otherwise, the system shall send an alert message to the patient's doctor
- If the patient does not submit the data before 10 a.m., an alert message shall be sent to the patient's doctor
- The alert message shall be sent in two minutes after the discovery of the patient's abnormal condition
- The alert message shall be sent by SMS (Short Message System), via telephone and email.

These requirements can be represented then as a state table or the series of paths built of required states and related transitions, such as when the system goes from the "waiting" state to the "send alert" state if there is no valid connection from a patient at or before 10 a.m.

From the BeMSET perspective, the important elements are:

- Contextual elements: the existence and execution of all required transition paths and their related states built from system behavior scenarios
- Quality elements: the existence of all required quality attributes of both states and transitions.

In the example, the contextual behavior is verified by examining all required transitions among states, while quality behavior is verified by measuring and evaluating related quality attributes, for which ISO/IEC 14598 (and its ISO/IEC 2504x) offers ready-to-use support. It seems justified, then, to verify whether this support could be extended to the evaluation of trustworthiness as the whole process in the context of BeMSET.

4.3.2.2.2 ISO/IEC 14598-3 Process for Developers

ISO/IEC 14589-3 [24] "provides requirements and recommendations for the practical implementation of software product evaluation when the evaluation is conducted in parallel with the development and carried out by the developer." From the perspective of BeMSET, the process (Fig. 4.7) corresponds rather to auto-evaluation by the service supplier prior to submitting the service to a certification organization.

The phases of the evaluation process for developers are defined as follows (from ISO 14598-3):

- "analysis of evaluation requirements which consists of identifying the quality requirements according to an agreed quality model"
- "specification of the evaluation which consists of determining the external measures and target measurement values (criteria for evaluation)"
- "design of the evaluation which consists of determining the internal measures and target measurement values (criteria for evaluation)"
- "execution of the evaluation which consists of collecting internal measurement values during development and comparing with target values (evaluation

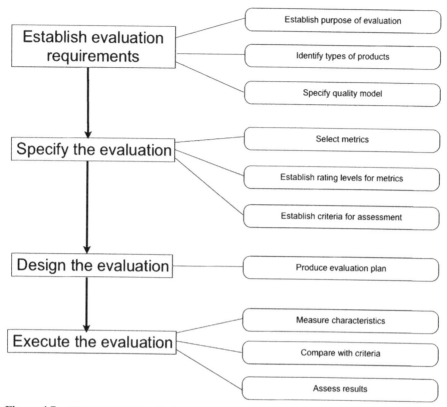

Figure 4.7   ISO/IEC 14598-1 evaluation process (adapted from [25]).

during development). Internal attribute values (quality indicators) are used to estimate end product quality"

- "conclusion of the evaluation which consists of collecting external measurement values when they become available and comparing with target values (evaluation of product quality)."

The first essential difference between evaluation of quality alone and evaluation of trustworthiness is the service (or software) life cycle phase in which the evaluation takes place.

Applying BeMSET requires the existence of a fully operational service, which means being far past internal quality definition and measurement stage. However, external quality may and should be perceived as "behavioral" as it applies to a running software or system that exhibits actions and reactions (services). Using this approach as a filtering mechanism to the process described in ISO/IEC 14598-3 automatically removes from it all activities related to internal quality, thus leaving the evaluation design and evaluation execution phases temporarily void.

The second essential difference between evaluation of quality and trustworthiness is the role of a verifier. In the ISO/IEC 14598 the developer *is* the verifier, while in auto-evaluation of trustworthiness using BeMSET, the developer becomes principally the user who evaluates both contextual and quality elements of the service, system, or software. Applying this observation to ISO/IEC 14598-3 indicates that the notion of "external quality" is too narrow and should be adjusted in all phases and activities that relate to it (analysis, specification, and conclusion of evaluation).

The third essential difference between evaluation of quality and trustworthiness is the notion of the "model." From the perspective of BeMSET, the quality model becomes a component of a larger model that also includes all the scenarios in which the system has to be trustworthy. The quality model should be used as an agreed-upon reference for structuring the quality requirements, and as such it can be a proprietary solution as well as a standardized one, like the model from ISO/IEC 9126 or ISO/IEC 25010. Additionally, keeping in mind that the ultimate objective of the analyzed process (of auto-evaluation) is the certification by an independent accrediting organization, the scenarios' parts of the overall model should come from the certification organization and be used as reference for granting the certification.

Despite being substantial, the aforementioned differences do not rule out the possibility of reusing the ISO/IEC 14598 (and ISO/IEC 2504x) process for developers in auto-evaluation of trustworthiness. After addressing them, the adapted process could consist the following five phases:

- Analysis of evaluation requirements, which consists of identifying all required transition paths, their related states, and corresponding quality requirements according to an agreed-upon BeMSET model
- Specification of the evaluation, which consists of determining the reference transition paths, required states, related quality measures, and target measurement values
- Design of the evaluation, which consists of determining execution sequences of evaluated paths, their order, recording and measurement techniques, and target quality measurement values
- Execution of the evaluation, which consists of executing and recording all specified paths and states and measuring quality values
- Conclusion of the evaluation, which consists of comparing recorded transition paths and states with their references, comparing quality measures with target values, and preparing the evaluation report.

ISO/IEC 14598-4 [26] contains "requirements, recommendations and guidelines for the measurement, assessment and evaluation of software product quality during acquisition of off-the-shelf software products, custom software products, or modifications to existing software products, in conjunction with the requirements of ISO/IEC 12207." From the perspective of BeMSET, the process (Fig. 4.8) corresponds to evaluation by the future user prior to the purchase of the service.

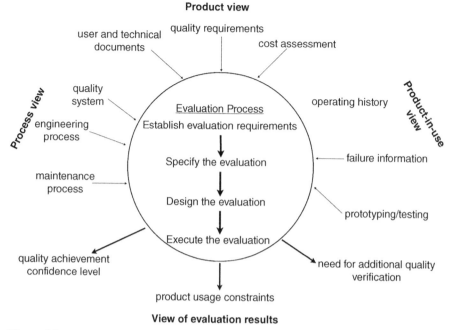

Figure 4.8 ISO/IEC 14598-4 evaluation process for acquirers (adapted from [26]).

The phases of the evaluation process for acquirers are defined as follows (direct quotation from ISO 14598-4):

- Establish evaluation requirements, define objectives and scope clearly. Identify:
  - what questions must be answered?
  - how rigorously should the evaluation be performed?
  - how complete are the inputs to the evaluation?
  - is additional evaluation planned for other phases of the project?
  - has any evaluation been done in previous phases of the project or by others?
  - what acquisition process is to be followed and how are evaluation input requirements communicated to the vendor?
- Specification of the evaluation. Once the requirements of the evaluation are understood:
  - select metrics that correlate to the characteristics of the software product and establish rating levels
  - select the most effective set of evaluation methods
  - establish procedures for summarizing the results of the evaluation of different quality characteristics and other aspects that contribute to the assessment of quality of a software product in a particular environment.

- Design of the evaluation. Prepare an evaluation plan describing the evaluation methods and the schedule of the evaluator actions. Identify the tie-points between evaluation activities and acquisition activities

- Execution of the evaluation. Conduct the selected evaluation activities, and analyze and record the results to determine the suitability of the software product(s). Analyze the impact of identified deficiencies and options to regulate the use of the existing software product. Draw conclusions with respect to the acceptability of the product and the ultimate decision to buy or not to buy.

The application of the analysis method used previously renders the following observations:

- In the phase of establishing evaluation requirements, the references to "phases of the project" are inapplicable and should be removed or modified to better adhere to the nature of trustworthiness evaluation

- In the phase of specification of the evaluation, the references to "metrics that correlate to the characteristics of the software product" are inapplicable and should be modified to better adhere to the nature of trustworthiness evaluation.

As the remaining phases of the ISO 14598 process for acquirers are applicable as they are, the adapted and simplified process could consist the following four phases:

- Establish evaluation requirements, define objectives and scope. Identify:
  - what questions must be answered from the point of view of evaluated service behavior and its quality?
  - how rigorously should the evaluation be performed?
  - how complete are the inputs to the evaluation?
  - has any evaluation been done prior to this acquisition or by others?
  - what acquisition process is to be followed and how are evaluation input requirements communicated to the vendor?

- Specification of the evaluation. Once the requirements of the evaluation are understood:
  - select reference transition paths, states and related quality measures and establish rating levels
  - select the most effective set of evaluation methods
  - establish procedures for summarizing the results of the evaluation

- Design of the evaluation. Prepare an evaluation plan describing the evaluation methods and the schedule of the evaluator actions. Identify the tie-points between evaluation activities and acquisition activities

- Execution of the evaluation. Conduct the selected evaluation activities, and analyze and record the results to determine the suitability of the software product(s). Analyze the impact of identified deficiencies and options to regulate the use of the existing service. Draw conclusions with respect to the acceptability of the service and the ultimate decision to buy or not to buy.

ISO/IEC 14598-5 [27] provides "requirements and recommendations for the practical implementation of software product evaluation when several parties need to understand, accept and trust evaluation results." From the perspective of BeMSET the process (Fig. 4.9) corresponds to evaluation of the service by the certification organization.

The phases of the process for evaluators are defined as follows (due to its original volume, the presented quotation from ISO 14598-5 has been shortened):

- Analysis of evaluation requirements:
  - expressing the extent of the coverage of the evaluation by the requester
  - explaining the extent of confidence and stringency of evaluation by the evaluator
  - agreeing on the evaluation requirements
- Specification of the evaluation based on the evaluation requirements and on the description of the product provided by the requester
  - specifying the measurements to be performed on the product and its components
  - verifying the specification produced with regards to the evaluation requirements
- Design of the evaluation which produces an evaluation plan on the basis of the evaluation
  - documenting evaluation methods and producing a draft plan
  - optimizing the evaluation plan
  - scheduling evaluation actions with regard to available resources
- Execution of the evaluation plan which consists of inspecting, modeling, measuring and testing the products and its components according to the evaluation plan
  - manage the product components provided by the requester
  - manage the data produced by the evaluation actions (including report and records
  - manage the tools to be used to perform the evaluation actions
  - manage evaluation actions performed outside the evaluator's premises
  - manage the requirements implied by the use of specific evaluation techniques.
- Conclusion of the evaluation, which consists of the delivery of the evaluation report and the disposal by the evaluator of the product evaluated as well as its components when they have been transmitted independently.

The application of the analysis method used previously indicates that this process can be applied to evaluation of trustworthiness after three minor adjustments:

- Replacement of the term " product" by the term "service"
- Replacement of the term " product and its components" by the term "service"
- Removing the term "modeling" from execution of the evaluation plan phase.

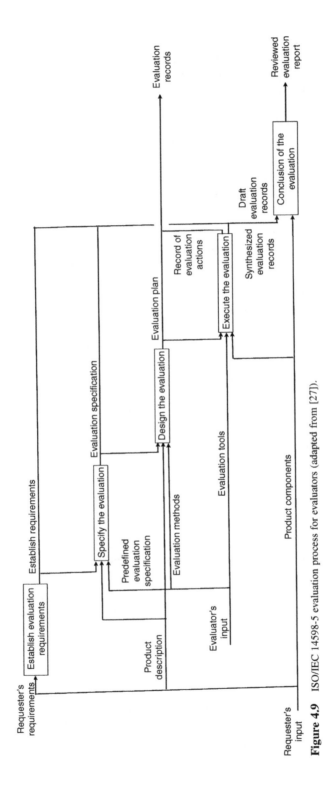

Figure 4.9 ISO/IEC 14598-5 evaluation process for evaluators (adapted from [27]).

In conclusion, the ISO/IEC 14598 (and ISO/IEC 2504x) evaluation offers a considerable support to the BeMSET-based evaluation of trustworthiness of software systems and services; however, not without sometimes substantial modifications.

The most essential identified modifications apply to the process for the developer, where the activities relating to internal quality and its measures should be removed; the evaluation requirements, specification, design, and execution should be focused on both contextual elements and quality elements rather than on quality alone; the model should be contextual quality rather than quality alone; and the role of the developer as verifier should be enhanced to cover the end-user perspective.

The modifications required for the process for the acquirers are relatively small and focus mostly on references to life cycle phases where the evaluation might take place and on direct references to evaluation of quality only.

The modifications required for the process for evaluators are reduced to replacing the term "product" by a more specific term, "service."

REFERENCES

1. Bishop M. *Computer Security: Art and Science*. Pearson Education, 2003.
2. "Trustworthiness," http://en.wikipedia.org/wiki/Trustworthiness.
3. Minnesota State Archives, http://www.mnhs.org/preserve/records/index.htm.
4. Dijkstra EW, Dahl OJ, Hoare CAR. *Structured Programming*. London: Academic Press, 1972.
5. Gill H. "High Confidence Software and Systems: Cyber-Physical Systems Progress Report: Semantics Perspective." In *Second Workshop on Event-based Semantics/IEEE RTAS; April 22–24, 2008*. Missouri: IEEE, 2008.
6. Avizienis A, Laprie JC, Randell, B. "Fundamental Concepts of Dependability." Technical Report 739; 2001. Department of Computing Science, University of Newcastle upon Tyne. Available at http://www.cs.cmu.edu/~garlan/17811/Readings/avizienis01_fund_concp_depend.pdf. Accessed May 16, 2013.
7. De Lemos R, Gacek C, Romanovsky A. "ICSE 2002 Workshop on Software Architectures for Dependable Systems (Workshop Summary)." *ACM Software Engineering Notes* 2003; 28(5).
8. Safford D. "The Need for TCPA." IBM Research. http://www.ibm.com. Accessed April 30, 2011.
9. Mundie C. "Trustworthy Computing: Microsoft White Paper." Available at http://download.microsoft.com/download/a/f/2/af22fd56-7f19-47aa-8167-4b1d73cd3c57/twc_mundie.doc. Accessed May 15, 2013.
10. DOD 5200.28 STD Trusted Computer System Evaluation Criteria. Department of Defense, National Computer Security Center, 1985.
11. Parnas, D. "Evaluation of Safety-Critical Software." *Communications of the ACM* 1990; 33(6):635–648.
12. Fedchak E, McGibbon T, Vienneau R. "Software Project Management for Software Assurance: A DACS State-of-the-Art-Report." Final report September 30, 2007. Air Force Research Lab, Griffiss. Report number 347617. Contract Number SP0700-98-D-4000. Available from https://buildsecurityin.us-cert.gov/bsi/dhs/906-BSI.html. Accessed May 15, 2013.

13. Goertzel KM, Winograd T, McKinley HL, Oh L, Colon M, McGibbon T, Fedchak E, Vienneau R. "Software Security Assurance: A State-of-the-Art-Report." DACS and IATAC joint report, July 31, 2007. Available at http://iac.dtic.mil/csiac/download/security.pdf. Accessed May 15, 2013.

14. Voas J, Agresti WW. "Software Quality from a Behavioral Perspective." *IT Professional* 2004; 6(4):46–50.

15. Yin G. "Practices and Thinking of the Models in Trustie Environment." International ABC Conference March 15, 2010; Tokyo, Japan. Available from www.trustie.net. Accessed May 15, 2013.

16. Hahnle R. "HATS: Highly Adaptable and Trustworthy Software Using Formal Models." International Symposium on Formal Methods for Components and Objects; October 23, 2008, Sofia-Antipolis. Available at http://www-sop.inria.fr/oasis/FMCO/2008/slides/FMCO2008-HATS-ReinerHahnle.pdf.

17. Phoomvuthisarn S. "An Architecture Approach to Dependable Trust-Based Service Systems." In *6th International Conference on Service Oriented Computing; December 1–5, 2008.* Sydney, Australia: ICSOC, 2008.

18. Suryn W. Yuan Y. "Trustworthiness of Software, the Challenge of the 21st Century." In *The International Standard Conference on Software Trustworthy Testing; December 28, 2009–January 2, 2010.* Beijing, China: BUPT, 2009.

19. Nami M. Suryn W. "From Requirements to Software Trustworthiness Using Scenarios and Finite State Machine." In *38th IECON conference; October 25–28, 2012.* Montreal, Canada: IEEE, 2012.

20. Wagne F, Schmuki R, Wagner T, Wolstenholme P. *"Modeling Software with Finite State Machines: A Practical Approach."* Boca Raton, FL: CRC Press, Taylor & Francis Group, 2006.

21. Behrens H. "Requirements Analysis and Prototyping Using Scenarios and Statecharts." ICSE 2002 Workshop; May 19–25, 2002, Orlando, Florida.

22. Merriam-Webster Dictionary, 2010.

23. "Mobius Glossary." Available at http://www-sop.inria.fr/marelle/Mobius/mobius.inria.fr/twiki/bin/view/Mobius/Glossary.html#T.

24. ISO/IEC 14598-3 Software Engineering—Product Evaluation—Part 3: Process for Developers. Geneva, Switzerland: International Organization for Standardization, 2000.

25. ISO/IEC 14598-1 Information Technology—Software Product Evaluation—Part 1: General Overview. Geneva, Switzerland: International Organization for Standardization, 1999.

26. ISO/IEC 14598-4 Software Engineering—Product Evaluation—Part 4: Process for Acquirers. Geneva, Switzerland: International Organization for Standardization, 1999.

27. ISO/IEC 14598-5 Information Technology—Software Product Evaluation—Part 5: Process for Evaluators. Geneva, Switzerland: International Organization for Standardization, 1998.

Appendix

Cost of Missing Quality: Case Studies

CASE 1: SOCIAL SECURITY TO PAY $500 MILLION TO 80,000 VICTIMS OF DATABASE ERROR

The Washington Post, one of the main newspapers in Washington D.C., cites in Reference 1 the case of a decision made based on a computer system error that caused 80,000 people to stop receiving their monthly benefits. It all started in 1996 when a federal law was promulgated to prevent justice fugitives from receiving any benefit from the government. In order to implement the measure, information from several government databases was compiled and, based on that, several thousand people had their benefits cancelled. The measure helped to capture several justice fugitives, but it also affected several people who had no criminal records. The article cites the case of Rosa Martinez, a resident from Redwood City California, whose monthly disability check was cancelled because the system had confused her records with those of another Rosa Martinez from Miami Florida. Apart from the hardships caused to people affected by the mistakes, the government faced several lawsuits that resulted in a considerable amount of vindications.

System Characteristics

The system described in the case study has typical components of a decision support system: data sources and a series of rules to analyze the data and recommend actions based on it. In this case, the quality of the data and the quality of the implemented algorithms to analyze it were not good enough to prevent problems for the system's owner.

Software Quality Engineering: A Practitioner's Approach, First Edition. Witold Suryn.
© 2014 the Institute of Electrical and Electronics Engineers, Inc.
Published 2014 by John Wiley & Sons, Inc.

Missing Quality

- Functionality. The system was not able to correctly perform its task. The data used in the system did not contain enough information to identify in a conclusive way every person in the databases. Due of this reason, when information from several data sources was aggregated, the implementers very likely had to resort to manual matching or heuristic algorithms.

- Testability. Even though the newspaper article does not mention this information, the outcome suggests that the system designers did not have enough elements to be able to correctly match the data from different data sources and be able to test different scenarios. Its lack of testability is very likely the cause of several of the errors when government policies changed.

Impact

Level B: Important economic or social impact.

- Privations to a vulnerable group of people. Arguably, the biggest impact caused by the missing quality in this system was the damage caused to the people who did not receive their benefits. The group of people who were entitled to receiving government benefits is comprised of the most vulnerable individuals in society, the elderly and the disabled. The disappearance of a source of income for these persons very likely caused them considerable damage.

- Liability and exposure costs. The government exposed itself to lawsuits by the affected people. These lawsuits caused a drain of financial resources that had to be rerouted from other sources, both to cover the costs of litigation and the indemnifications.

- Correction costs. Apart from the financial costs associated with the legal actions, the government had to dedicate resources to fix and verify the decisions made by the system, to prevent further errors and fix the existing ones.

- Unhappy customers. Even though in this case the error did not come from a business, there were unhappy customers, or in this case, unhappy citizens. The error might have political impact as the knowledge about the mistake might have led to loss of confidence in the government.

CASE 2: VA WRONGLY TELLS VETERANS THEY HAVE A FATAL DISEASE

The Federal Computer Week Magazine [2] wrote, in an article dated August 26, 2009, of a case in the Veterans Affairs Department of the United States (an organization that administers benefits for military veterans), where an error in a decision support system caused 1,200 veterans to be wrongly informed that they had acquired a fatal disease. The following text taken from the magazine describes the problem:

> The Veterans Affairs Department sent electronically generated letters last week that wrongly told as many as 1,200 veterans they have been diagnosed with the fatal Lou Gehrig's neurological disease, according to Jim Bunker, president of the National Gulf War Resource Center, a veteran's services nonprofit group. The VA did not comment on the cause of the mistake. Bunker said it happened due to years of misapplication of computer medical coding. Bunker said that for many years, the VA applied a medical code to refer to undiagnosed neurological disorders. Several years ago, he said, VA expanded the code category to include amyotrophic lateral sclerosis, commonly called Lou Gehrig's disease. Recently, the VA determined ALS to be a service-connected disability and generated automatic letters to all veterans whose records included the code for the disease. However, since the coding contained both ALS and undiagnosed neurological disorders, some of those letters were erroneous, Bunker said.

System Characteristics

The system described in the article is a medical decision support system. The error itself was not caused by a problem in the computer code or the data analysis algorithms, but by a human mistake in the way the data was being categorized. As mentioned in the case description, the problem was that two different diseases were being saved in the databases as if they were the same.

Missing Quality

- User error protection. The root cause was that the system allowed an incorrect categorization of the data by the people responsible for entering the data.
- Suitability. The category used to "tag" the new disease was not "suitable" to tag the new disease. In this case the lack of suitability was not a defect in the software, but in the data. Since all decision support systems rely heavily on databases, they are particularly vulnerable to database errors.

Impact

Level C: Significant impact on human life.

- The system gave incorrect information to clients in sensitive matters. The impact of the lack of reliability in this case did not financially affect the organization that caused the error, but it affected the well being of the recipients of the letters, since they received wrong information about their health.

CASE 3: SEVERAL PERSONS DIE DUE TO A BUG IN SOFTWARE IN THE THERAC-25 MACHINE

The Therac-25 machine is a case of an industrial support system that had lethal consequences due to errors in software. The Therac-25 was a radiation machine used in hospitals to perform radiation therapy and create X-ray pictures of patients. It was involved in a series of accidents that caused deaths and severe injuries to people who were exposed to the machine. The following description of the problem was taken from Reference 3:

The machine offered two modes of radiation therapy:

- direct electron-beam therapy, which delivered low doses of high-energy (5 MeV to 25 MeV) electrons over short periods of time
- megavolt X-ray therapy, which delivered X-rays produced by colliding high-energy (25 MeV) electrons into a "target"

When operating in direct electron-beam therapy mode, a low-powered electron beam was emitted directly from the machine then spread to safe concentration using scanning magnets. When operating in megavolt X-ray mode, the machine was designed to rotate four components into the path of the electron beam: a target, which converted the electron beam into X-rays; a flattening filter, which spread the beam out over a larger area; a set of movable blocks (also called a collimator), which shaped the X-ray beam; and an X-ray ion chamber, which measured the strength of the beam.

The accidents occurred when the high-power electron beam was activated instead of the intended low power beam, and without the beam spreader plate rotated into place. The machine's software did not detect that this had occurred, and therefore did not prevent the patient from receiving a potentially lethal dose of radiation. The high-powered electron beam struck the patients with approximately 100 times the intended dose of radiation, causing a feeling described by patient Ray Cox as "an intense electric shock." It caused him to scream and run out of the treatment room. Several days later, radiation burns appeared and the patients showed the symptoms of radiation poisoning. In three cases, the injured patients died later from radiation poisoning.

System Characteristics

The Therac-25 machine is a specific example of a system in which one of the parts is an industrial support system. In this case the software part was responsible for controlling the hardware parts of the machine and the malfunction of the software had lethal consequences.

Missing Quality

- Accuracy. The main cause of the accidents was the lack of accuracy in the doses of radiation that the patients had to receive. As mentioned in the problem description, the patients received up to ten times the amount of radiation that they should have received.

- Testability. According to a study made about the case cited in Reference 4, a commission formed to investigate the case found that one of the main causes of the problems was that the software was designed in such a way that it was impossible to test. It is also mentioned that the machine was never tested with the exact configuration of hardware and software where it was going to run until it was already in the hospital

- Fault tolerance. The machine failed only when a nonstandard sequence of keys was pressed. This incorrect sequence of keys can be considered as a "fault" from the part of the operator, so the software was not prepared to handle or "tolerate" this kind of errors.

Impact

Level A: Death of human being.

- Physical damage to patients. The machine caused radiation poisoning and burns to several patients exposed to it.

- Death of patients. The deaths of six people were proved to be directly caused by the machine.

- Investigation costs. Several experts of different fields had to be engaged in the investigations that led to the determination of the causes of the problems with the machine.

- Recall costs. After it was confirmed that machine could harm the people it was supposed to help, all the Therac-25 machines were recalled by the manufacturer.

CASE 4: SMELT PLANT SHUTS DOWN DUE TO SOFTWARE BUG

The Website of the computer science department of the Tel Aviv University [4] cites a note in a New Zealand newspaper that describes how a smelting plant was shut down due to errors in software. The exact transcription of the problem is the following:

> A computer software error at the Tiwai Point aluminum smelter in Southland, New Zealand at midnight on New Year's Eve 1997 caused more than $AU 1 million of damage. The software error was the failure to account for leap years (and considering a 366th day in the year to be invalid), causing 660 process control computers to shut down and the smelting pots to cool. The same problem occurred two hours later at Comalco's Bell Bay smelter in Tasmania (which is two hours behind New Zealand). The general manager of operations for New Zealand Aluminum Smelters, David Brewer, said "It

was a complicated problem and it took quite some time [until midafternoon] to find the cause. (Originally from *The New Zealand Herald*, January 8, 1997, and *The Dominion*, in Wellington, New Zealand).

System Characteristics

The system in this case study was responsible for controlling the operations of a smelting plant. It can be classified in the control systems branch of the industrial support systems. According to the information presented in the note, the main cause of the problem was incorrect date handling in the internal system's calendar.

Missing Quality

- Accuracy. In this case study, the root cause of the problem was the lack of accuracy in date handling in the software that controlled the smelting plant. There are not many details available about the causes of the error, but it is very likely that the software programmers had implemented their own date format, instead of using an existing and tested one.
- Fault tolerance. The whole system was affected by a problem in the handling of the dates. While it is very hard to prevent unknown errors, there are development techniques, such as defensive programming, that can help to minimize the effect of faults. In this case, it is unlikely that such a technique was used.

Impact

Level B: Dramatic economic impact on the company.

- Financial loss. The company lost $AU 1 million due to the problem.

CASE 5: VOYAGES-SNCF.COM

Voyages-sncf.com is a popular e-business site in France. It's used by 25% of the French population. On November 20, 2008, this site was inaccessible for 30 hours. The problem occurred after a new version of the site was deployed [5].

Missing Quality

- Fault tolerance. It is probable that the new version of the system was not able to handle errors; this problem caused the site to crash due to events that normally would not bring down the complete site. As a result of this, many customers were affected and the site lost revenue.

- Installability. Again, it is probable that installing a new version did not go as required, creating a nonfunctional instance of the system.
- Coexistence. One of the frequent reasons for "explosions" of new releases of the software is forgetting that the software usually resides on an operating system that contains other applications. The modifications in new releases sometimes put in conflict functionalities that worked well before the modifications.

Impact

Level C: Critical economic impact.

- 30 hours of downtime, considerable revenue lost, dissatisfied customers.

CASE 6: EBAY

On June 14, 1999 the eBay web site was down for 22 hours, and 2.3 million bids failed. The web site claims being a victim of first "hardware failure" and after that "network failure" [6].

Missing Quality

- Fault tolerance. The system was not able to properly react to failures and continue working.

Impact

Level C: Critical economic impact.

- 2.3 million bids failed.

CASE 7: A SOFTWARE GLITCH ERASED THE WAREHOUSE'S EXISTENCE TO THE BRITISH FOOD RETAILER SAINSBURY'S

In October 2004, the automated distribution system of the British food retailer Sainsbury's had a problem that affected the distribution of merchandise between stores. The problem resulted in the system sending the merchandise to wrong locations. The company had to disregard the system and lost the investment of $526 million it had made in it [7].

Missing Quality

- Accuracy. The lack of accuracy in the data coming out of the system caused the deliveries to be sent to incorrect locations.

Impact

Level B: Major financial impact.

- $526 million lost.

CASE 8: HIT THE WRONG KEY, BECOME A VERB . . .

Pablo Davila lost at least $207 million of Codelco, a state-owned Chilean company by typing the wrong financial transaction into his computer. He typed "buy" when he says he meant to type "sell." Now, all of Chile is obsessed with the mistake that cost 0.5% of Chile's GNP and the new word "davilar" is a verb that is ". . . loosely translated as 'to botch things up miserably.'" Integral text from Reference 8.

Missing Quality

- Operability, user error protection. The system does not support the user to operate and control the software, and if he or she makes an accidental manipulation, the system does not prevent it from happening.

Impact

Level B: Human lives and financial impact.

- Lost at least $207 million.

CASE 9: ONLINE BANKING SYSTEM FAILURE

Three of the twelve largest banks in Japan merged. The results were not pretty, including "more than 30,000 transaction errors and 2.5 million delayed debits" and "2.5 million of the 3 million automatic debits scheduled to be processed on 1 Apr. 2002, including utility and credit card bills, couldn't be made on that day."

The problem was that each of the banks ran a different system (Hitachi, IBM, and Fujitsu, although no software was mentioned). They built some integration glue, but it did not work. About 30,000 incorrect double withdrawals and about 5,000 double deposits were found and corrected.

According to the bank, "the overall accumulation of delayed transaction would need the whole week to finish." Integral text from [9].

Missing Quality

* Interoperability.

Impact

Level B: Critical economic impact on Japan's banking system.

* About 30,000 incorrect double withdrawals
* About 5,000 double deposits
* Accumulation of delayed transaction.

CASE 10: MAJOR COMPUTER FAILURE AT HSBC BANK

From August 15 to August 22, 2011, 4 million U.S. customers of HSBC Bank could not use their debit cards or their deposits were delayed [10].

Missing Quality

* Fault tolerance
* Maturity.

Impact

Level D: Negligible economic or social impact.

* Customer satisfaction lost.

CASE 11: BOEING 787 NETWORKING ISSUES

Boeing's new 787 Dreamliner passenger jet may have serious security vulnerability in its onboard computer networks that could allow passengers to access the plane's control systems, according to the U.S. Federal Aviation Administration. The computer network in the Dreamliner's passenger compartment, designed to give passengers in-flight Internet access, is connected to the plane's control, navigation, and communication systems, an FAA report reveals. The revelation is causing concern in security circles because the physical connection of the networks makes the plane's control systems vulnerable to hackers. A more secure design would physically separate the two computer networks. Boeing has said that it is aware of the issue and has designed a solution it will test shortly [11].

System Characteristic

The described system is an airplane network system. It performs the functions of giving passengers in-flight Internet access, but is connected to the plane's control, navigation, and communication systems.

Missing Quality

- Security. No isolation between the plane control network and the entertainment network. This situation could lead to possible failures or faults in the network system and allow access to the plane's control systems by passengers.

Impact

Level A: Probable loss of human lives.

- Possible airplane operation failures
- Flight pilot may lose airplane control
- Could lead to loss of human lives.

CASE 12: BUFFER OVERFLOW IN BERKELEY UNIX FINGER DAEMON

The first Internet worm (the so-called Morris Worm) infected between 2,000 and 6,000 computers in less than a day by taking advantage of a buffer overflow. The specific code is a function in the standard input/output library routine called gets(), designed to get a line of text over the network. Unfortunately, gets() has no provision to limit its input, and an overly large input allows the worm to take over any machine to which it can connect.

Programmers respond by attempting to stamp out the gets() function in working code, but they refuse to remove it from the C programming language's standard input/output library, where it remains to this day [12].

System Characteristic

Personal or business computers connected to the Internet.

Missing Quality

- Security. Serious vulnerability in the software library that allows malicious software to take control computers.

Impact

Level C: Some significant economic impact.

- Infection by a computer worm
- Possible data theft
- Possibility of malicious deeds.

CASE 13: AT&T NETWORK OUTAGE

A bug in a new release of the software that controls AT&T's #4ESS long distance switches caused these mammoth computers to crash when they received a specific message from one of their neighboring machines—a message that the neighbors send out when they recover from a crash.

One day a switch in New York crashed and rebooted, causing its neighboring switches to crash, then their neighbors' neighbors, and so on. Soon, 114 switches were crashing and rebooting every six seconds, leaving an estimated 60 thousand people without long distance service for nine hours. The fix: engineers load the previous software release [13].

System Characteristic

Telecommunication long distance switches.

Missing Quality

- Recoverability. Inability to recover automatically from a crash.
- Maturity. Inability to stay in functional mode after receiving a special message.

Impact

Level B: Continuous usage of the system.

- Long-distance service disruption.

CASE 14: THE PING OF DEATH

A lack of sanity checks and error handling in the IP fragmentation reassembly code makes it possible to crash a wide variety of operating systems by sending a malformed "ping" packet from anywhere on the Internet. Most obviously affected are computers running Windows, which lock up and display the so-called "blue screen of death" when they receive these packets. But the attack also affects many Macintosh and Unix systems as well [14].

System Characteristic

Computer base communication system.

Missing Quality

- Fault tolerance. Operating systems unable to continue to operate after receiving malformed messages.

Impact

Level C: Continuous usage and possible significant economic loss.

- Vulnerability to malicious attack.

CASE 15: TELECOMMUNICATIONS FAILURE ISOLATES LIBERIA

"Monrovia—Liberia, entered on Wednesday the seventh day of a major breakdown in its telecommunications facilities, isolating the country from the international community and impeding local transactions." Telephone, fax, and telex services of the Liberia Telecommunication Corporation went mute, leaving internal and external communications to two private phone and Internet companies. The managing director of the corporation, Charles Roberts, told PANA that the breakdown was due to loss of essential data from the memory bank of the main central processing unit of the switching exchange. Roberts admitted the company's equipment was near obsolete, but rejected claims that neglect of maintenance had caused a collapse in the facility [15].

Missing Quality

- Fault tolerance. Operating systems unable to stay up after data loss.
- Suitability. Ability to backup data used for system processing.

Impact

Level A: Disastrous economic or social impact.

- Major economic impact on Liberia
- Business and bank activities paralyzed
- Local and international institutions practically paralyzed.

CASE 16: FAILURE OF LONDON AMBULANCE DISPATCH SYSTEM

In 1992, the failure of the London ambulance system's information management system resulted in deaths of several people, since no ambulance arrived on time. The following description of the situation was taken from Reference 16:

> After a whole slew of issues, including a project cancellation and re-design, a software system got developed and was deployed the morning of October 26, 1992. Just a few hours later, however, problems began to arise. The AVLS was unable to keep track of the ambulances and their statuses in the system. It began sending multiple units to some locations and no units to other locations. The efficiency with which it assigned vehicles to call locations was substandard. The system began to generate such a great quantity of exception messages on the dispatchers' terminals that calls got lost. The problem was compounded when people called back additional times because the ambulances they were expecting did not arrive. As more and more incidents were entered into the system, it became increasingly clogged. The next day, the LAS switched back to a part-manual system, and shut down the computer system completely when it quit working altogether eight days later.

System Characteristics

The London dispatch system can be classified as a hybrid between an information management system and a telecommunications control system, because it manages ambulance information and it has remote communication capabilities to allow communications between ambulances and central.

Missing Quality

- Accuracy. The LAS was not able to adequately track and manage of the ambulances and the service calls locations.

Impact

Level B: Major financial impact.

- Loss of human lives. According to Reference 16, at least 46 people died who could have been saved.

- Financial loss. The system was shut down completely, which caused complete investment loss.

CASE 17: TORONTO PUBLIC HEALTH COMPUTER ACCIDENTALLY ERASES RECORDS

The Toronto Star reported in its March 10, 2003, issue [17] a problem in an information management system that caused the loss of medical information. The problem description is the following:

> A computer fault may have accidentally erased the immunization records of thousands of Toronto school children, the city's public health department fears. Last April, the department discovered that its immunization records information system was erasing files from among 425,000 student records, Dr. Barbara Yaffe, associate medical officer of health, said. "It appears it was randomly erasing files—and we don't know how many."

The department tried to obtain technical help from the provincial health ministry, but its technicians were among the 45,000 Ontario civil servants taking part in a 54-day strike that spring.

System Characteristic

The described system is a medical information management system. Such systems are common in the hospitals and clinics and are used to make decisions regarding a patient's health.

Missing Quality

- Reliability. The system could not guarantee the integrity of the stored information.
- Functionality. Due to its lack of integrity, the system was not able to accomplish is main task.

Impact

Level C: Minor impact on human lives.

- Rework costs. The missing data had to be reentered manually in the system; in addition, all the information had to be verified to ensure record accuracy.
- Possible impact to the health of the affected children. Due to missing information, some children could have been vaccinated more than one time, which could have had negative effects on their health.

REFERENCES

1. Gowen A. "Social Security to Pay $500 Million to 80,000 Victims of Database." *The Washington Post*, August 12, 2009.
2. Lipowicz A. "VA Wrongly Tells Vets They Have a Fatal Disease." *Federal Computer Week*, August 26, 2009. Available at http://fcw.com/articles/2009/08/26/va-erroneously -informs-vets-of-fatal-disease-diagnosis.aspx. Accessed May 10, 2013.
3. "An Investigation of the Therac-25 Accidents." *IEEE Computer* 1993; 26(7):18–41.
4. "Software Horror Stories." Entry 55. Available at http://www.cs.tau.ac.il/~nachumd/ horror.html. Accessed May 10, 2013.
5. "Retour à la normale pour Voyages-sncf.com." *01net*, November 20, 2008.
6. Clark T. "eBay Online Again after 14-Hour Outage." *CNET*, August 6, 1999.
7. Leveson N. *Safeware: System Safety and Computers*. Addison-Wesley, 1995.
8. Wayner P. "Hit the Wrong Key, Become a Verb." *Risk Digest* 1994; 15(66).
9. Ishikawa I. "Online Banking System Failure in a Big Way." *Risk Digest* 2002; 22(3).
10. Osborne H. "HSBC Computer Failure Leaves Customers Short of Cash." *The Guardian*, November 4, 2011.
11. Zetter K. "FAA: Boeing's New 787 May Be Vulnerable to Hacker Attack." *Wired*, April 1, 2008.
12. Panettieri JC. "Who Let the Worms Out?" *eWEEK*, March 12, 2001.
13. "Software Glitch Cripples AT&T." *Telephony*, January 22, 1990.
14. Erickson J. *Hacking: The Art of Exploitation*, 2nd ed. No Starch Press, 2008.
15. "Telecommunications Failure Isolates Liberia." *Panafrican News Agency*, November 1, 2000.
16. Dalcher D. "Disaster in London: The LAS Case Study." In *ECBS 99 IEEE Conference and Workshop on Engineering of Computer-Based Systems, March 7–12, 1999*, pp. 41–52.
17. Smith C. "Health Records Feared Erased." *Toronto Star*, March 10, 2003.

Index

Software Quality Engineering: A Practitioner's Approach, First Edition. Witold Suryn.
© 2014 the Institute of Electrical and Electronics Engineers, Inc.
Published 2014 by John Wiley & Sons, Inc.